Special Needs in the General Classroom

500+ Teaching Strategies for Differentiating Instruction

Third Edition

Dedication

To my all my students who taught me so much.
You made me a better teacher.

Special Needs in the General Classroom

500+ Teaching Strategies for Differentiating Instruction

Third Edition

Susan Gingras Fitzell, M.Ed.

Cogent Catalyst Publications

Printed in the United States of America.

Library of Congress Cataloging-in-publication Data
    Fitzell, Susan Gingras
    Includes bibliographic references
    ISBN 978-1-932995-36-7 (pbk.)
    1. Teaching Teams 2. Classroom Management

Fitzell, Susan Gingras.
Special Needs in the General Classroom:
500+ Teaching Strategies for Differentiating Instruction

Includes bibliographical references.

If you have questions or would like customized school in-service or ongoing consultation, contact:

Susan Gingras Fitzell
PO Box 6182
Manchester, NH 03108-6182
603-625-6087 or 210-473-2863
sfitzell@susanfitzell.com
www.susanfitzell.com

GET YOUR BONUS RESOURCES HERE:

http://Bonus367.susanfitzell.com

TABLE OF CONTENTS

ℬ CHAPTER 4 ℜ

CREATING CARING INCLUSIVE COMMUNITIES 89

ℬ CHAPTER 5 ℜ

TOOLS AND FORMS THAT SUPPORT SUCCESS 103

READ FIRST

This book is designed to help you meet the challenges of teaching in an inclusive classroom. You will find techniques for collaboration between special education staff and classroom teachers, as well as practical, proven ways to differentiate your teaching methods and materials to increase the effectiveness of your instruction and meet Individual Education Plan (IEP) adaptations in the general classroom without reducing content.

You will find teaching approaches, games, activities, and examples of adaptations to help your students become more successful in the inclusive classroom. These approaches and techniques work for ALL youth in the inclusive classroom and are critical for students with special needs.

A motto that works:

GOOD FOR ALL, CRITICAL FOR DIFFERENT LEARNERS!

PREFACE

A Matter of Perspective

For over 25 years I have been working with students with learning differences. Sixteen of those years have been in public education. From my experience and knowledge, based on extensive research on learning disabilities, brain-based learning, personality type, learning styles, and multiple intelligences, I propose the following as points of consideration and discussion:

- I firmly believe that many problems labeled as "learning disabilities" are actually learning differences. If we pay attention to students' learning styles, multiple intelligences, and brain-based teaching techniques, we will find ourselves more successful with all learners.

- Many students who do well in high school with minimal effort struggle in college because they lack the necessary study skills, organizational skills, and memory strategies needed for the types of careers these bright young people are working toward: law, engineering, medicine, etc.

- My approach to teaching diverse learners in the classroom is to meet their needs in the least obvious way possible so they don't stick out as "different," and to create a learning environment where all students, including the gifted, benefit from the experience.

"Many educationally 'different' children are bright and potentially talented. Few, if any, are 'unteachable,' but there is ample proof that plunging them abruptly into the chilly, analytic waters of mainstream instructional practices is a prescription for failure, frustration, and a high dropout rate. The schools have three choices:

1. *Keep the traditional 'standards' and continue to cram youth into them. Let prisons and the welfare system handle the overflow.*

2. *Throw out the standards.*

3. *Maintain the goals represented by the standards, but prepare students more effectively. Expand the schedule of expectation and the teaching methods to honor young people's latent abilities.*

The first two alternatives should be unthinkable. We are left with the third."

Excerpted from Endangered Minds by Jane M. Healy, Ph.D. (Healy, 1999)

❧ CHAPTER 1 ☙

Good for All, Critical for Different Learners

Introduction

I wrote the first edition of this book in 1998. At that time, my children were young and I was teaching full-time as a special education teacher in an inclusive classroom. Our classroom was heterogeneously grouped and, in most instances, students with mild to moderate special needs and learning disabilities thrived in mixed ability classrooms.

In Chapter 1, I share my thoughts on learning differences. Very little is changed in my thinking. I not only have the perspective of special education co-teacher teaching in Londonderry, New Hampshire, I now have a perspective deepened by my work coaching teachers in differentiated, inclusive, and often, co-taught classrooms all over the country.

I also have a son and a daughter who have navigated the public school system successfully, utilizing their strengths and overcoming their weaknesses with the very same strategies that I share in this book. My son has Central Auditory Processing Disorder as well as a form of dyslexia. I was told more than once in his school life that he did not belong in honors classes, that he was an overachiever and shouldn't be where he is; and one teacher went as far as to say that if he continued to push himself so hard to achieve beyond his ability level that he may end up in a mental institution. So, I have a mother's perspective of how students are often limited because of teacher expectations versus their own motivation. My son earned a scholarship to engineering school, graduated with a degree in mechanical engineering and is gainfully employed as a design engineer.

My experiences as a teacher, a mother, a coach, and a consultant have provided me with a very clear understanding of what works and what doesn't work in a differentiated, inclusive classroom. I invite you to have an open mind in your exploration of differentiated instruction and meeting the needs of different learners as you read through this book. Have fun with it.

Why Change Mindsets About Student Potential?

I started teaching in 1980 and, over the years, I became increasingly aware of the large number of students who were labeled special needs who probably did not need nor deserve that stigma and lifelong label. A consequence of that label is often a blow to the student's self-esteem.

So often, I would work with students who, on-record, had learning disabilities, yet, when they were given strategies that honored their learning style, could be successful. I often thought that these students were unjustly labeled simply because at the secondary level, we primarily teach to verbal linguistic auditory learners.

John's second grade teacher suggested to his parents that he had Attention Deficit with Hyperactivity Disorder (ADHD). His parents, unwilling to wait for the public school evaluation process took it upon themselves to have him evaluated. He was diagnosed with Central Auditory Processing Disorder. In the fourth grade, his parents and teachers noticed that his reading test scores were going down.

Although the teachers weren't too concerned at the time, his parents once again had an outside evaluation done by a behavioral optometrist. It was determined that he had significant under-convergence of his eyes. His parents provided him with vision therapy. In one summer, he went from reading "Magic Tree House" books to "The Lord of the Rings".

As John went through the school system on a 504 plan, his parents supplemented his education with metacognitive strategies provided by SuperCamp, sent him to immersion language programs during the summer to prepare for high school world language classes, and engaged an academic coach to support him in developing writing skills and preparing for state tests.

John, who by traditional academic standards would have been considered a candidate for special education without the support his parents provided, was able to be successful in school because he had a lifetime of 'interventions'. Those 'interventions' responded to his academic struggles in ways that honored his strengths and learning style.

This student is now in an engineering program at private university on a scholarship he earned because of his success in honors level and advanced placement course work in high school. John's eye-doctor, fifth grade teacher and academic coach expressed that what John accomplished was amazing considering his Central Auditory Processing Disorder (CAPD) and vision issues.

Instructional leaders and educators may not be able to provide special camps or private coaches for students; however, the moral of this story is: A student who *without interventions,* would have started second grade in the lowest reading group and would have stayed tracked at that level through his school career would not be where he is today if his parents had not intervened. Providing intervention strategies to students, double dosing instruction (as John had with camps and tutors), frequently monitoring progress, and adjusting interventions will allow other students to have the same opportunity as John to reach the stars.

With this strategy book, I am calling upon teachers to change mindsets in a way that breaks the traditional mode of verbal linguistic auditory teaching at the middle and high school level and embrace differentiated instruction and respect for student learning styles. Teachers will see that students can be more successful than we ever thought possible because they haven't been cast out of our general education classrooms, placed in pull-out and self-contained programs and consequently labeled "those kids who can't..."

When we label students "special education" we sentence them to lower expectations and diminish their chance to achieve at their greatest potential. I know this for a fact because, until my high school forced inclusion of students with special needs into the general education classroom, where expectations and demands were higher than in self-contained classrooms, students with special needs rarely went to college. Despite constant encouragement, countless attaboys, and transition searches for the 'right job', students achieved so much less than they were capable of. I was personally part of the generation of teachers who taught self-contained classrooms and dumbed-down the curriculum so students with special needs could simply get through school. We knew no better at the time. We believed it was the right thing to do.

What I learned, personally and professionally, through my experience co-teaching in inclusive classrooms is that I spent years underestimating my students and therefore had a part in sentencing them to a lifetime of less. When students remain in the general education classroom and benefit from the expertise of a general education teacher and have the supports of differentiated lesson plans, interventions, and, when possible, co-teaching, students who might otherwise be labeled at risk, slow learners, learning disabled, or special ed achieve more than they will ever achieve in low-level classes where the expectation is "they can't."

The School House Model

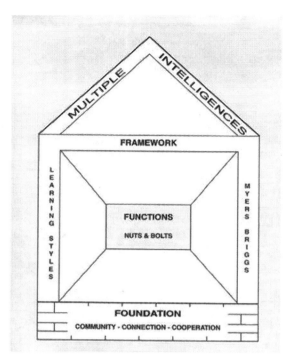

Foundation

In setting up an individual classroom or even an entire school, it is best to look at the School House Model. The base of the model is the foundation – **community, connection, and cooperation.** Many schools and individual classrooms forget this foundation and then wonder why students can't work or learn together. It is important to have a strong foundation. We can look at Maslow's hierarchy of needs and see that four out of the five needs (physiological, safety, social, and self-esteem) are concerned with this area of foundation.

Framework

The framework for the individual classroom or entire school should be based on an understanding of how students learn based on current brain and educational research. If the teacher and students understand the differences in how they learn and make decisions based on that understanding, then they can progress to the self-actualization need that Maslow describes, and learning can happen (Bell, 2005).

Functions

The center of the School House Model is the functions, or nuts and bolts. This is the actual curriculum and academic elements that should be taught. However, if the teacher or school only focuses on the functions and disregards both the foundation and framework, then the student will have a difficult time learning and retaining the knowledge presented.

When training teachers, if they are only presented with the functions and do not have a foundation and framework, they will not be able to create new ideas and lesson plans on their own, but will only be able to try and replicate the functions that have been presented to them.

Differentiated Instruction

Differentiated instruction (Burnett, n.d.) is an approach to planning in which lessons are taught to the entire class while meeting the individual needs of each child. This is accomplished by consistently planning lessons using strategies that meet the needs of all learners in the classroom. The content, process (instructional strategies), and product are how the teacher meets the needs of all the students. The teacher determines the process per the students' readiness level, interests, and learning profile.

EACH LESSON
- Has a definite goal for all students.
- Includes a variety of teacher techniques aimed at reaching students at all levels.
- Considers students' learning styles in presentation of lessons.
- Involves all students in the lesson using questioning aimed at different levels of thinking.
- Challenges students with respectful work based on their individual readiness level.
- Provides choice in the method students will use to demonstrate understanding.
- Accepts that different methods are of equal value.
- Evaluates students based on their individual differences.

STEPS:

1. *Identify Goals:*
   - Content – What do all students need to understand? Separate content from process.
   - Individual student objectives.

2. *Method of Presentation:*
   - Content is presented using methods that facilitate all students gaining varying degrees of knowledge based on their level of understanding.
   - Cognizant of individual student learning style and multiple intelligences.
   - Attending to level of cognitive domain – Bloom's Taxonomy (questioning techniques critical).
   - Differentiated participation based on each student's skill level.
   - Adaptations may be necessary to the environment, the materials, and the mode of presenting the information.

3. *Method of Student Practice:*
   - Assignments based on each student's needs.
   - Consistent with learning style of student.
   - Appropriate for level of cognitive ability – Bloom's Taxonomy.
   - Differentiated participation based on each student's skill level.

4. *Method of Evaluation:*
   - Linked to identified goals.
   - Considers learning styles of student.
   - Considers level of cognitive ability – Bloom's Taxonomy.
   - Differentiated participation based on each student's skill level.

Theory: Multiple Intelligences

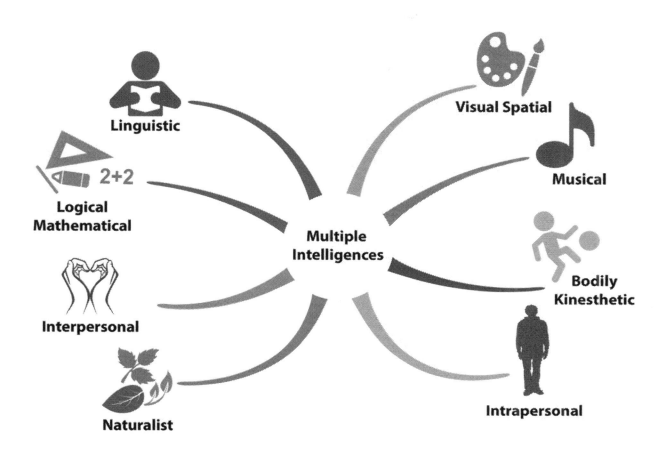

Psychologist Howard Gardner ("What is a Gifted Child? Trying to define the beast," 2007) identified the following distinct types of intelligence in his book, *Frames of Mind*. Per his theory, all people possess eight distinct sets of capabilities. Gardner emphasizes that these capabilities/intelligences work together, not in isolation. The intelligences, including his newest finding, the Naturalist, are:

Linguistic: Young people with this kind of intelligence use words effectively, either orally or in writing. They enjoy writing, reading, telling stories, or doing crossword puzzles.

Logical-Mathematical: Children have the capacity to use numbers effectively and to reason well. They are interested in patterns, categories, and relationships. They are drawn to arithmetic problems, strategy games, and experiments.

Bodily Kinesthetic: Children with this capability are experts in using their whole body to express ideas and feelings. They are good with their hands. These kids process knowledge through bodily sensations. They are often athletic, dancers, or good at crafts such as sewing or woodworking.

Spatial: These young people think in images and pictures. They may be fascinated with mazes or jigsaw puzzles, or spend free time drawing, building with construction sets, or inventing.

Musical: Musical students have the capacity to perceive, discriminate, transform, and express musical forms. They often spend time singing or drumming to themselves. They are usually quite aware of sounds others may miss. These kids are often discriminating listeners.

Interpersonal: These students have the ability to perceive and make distinctions in the moods, intentions, motivations, and feelings of other people. They are often leaders among their peers, who are good at communicating and responding to others' feelings.

Intrapersonal: These students are insightful and self-aware. They can adapt to their environment based on their understanding of themselves. These students may be shy. They are very aware of their own emotions, strengths, and limitations, and have the capacity for self-discipline.

Naturalist: The core of the Naturalist intelligence is the human ability to recognize plants, animals, and other parts of the natural environment, like clouds or rocks. These students have the ability to identify and classify patterns in nature. These students are sensitive to changes in the weather or are adept at distinguishing nuances between large quantities of similar objects.

Existentialist: Students who learn in the context of where humankind stands in the "big picture" of existence. They ask "Why are we here?" and "What is our role in the world?" This intelligence is seen in the discipline of philosophy.

Multiple Intelligences (MI) cannot be an educational end in itself. MI is, rather, a powerful tool that can help us to achieve educational ends more effectively. From my vantage point, MI is most useful for two educational ends:

1. *It allows us to plan educational programs that will enable children to realize desired end states (for example, the musician, the scientist, the civic-minded person);*

2. *It helps us to reach more children who are trying to understand important theories and concepts in the disciplines.*

So long as materials are taught and assessed in only one way, we will only reach a certain kind of child. But everything can be taught in several ways. The more that we can match youngsters to congenial approaches of teaching, learning, and assessing, the more likely it is that those youngsters will achieve educational success.

~Howard Gardner in an interview with Ronnie Durie (Durie, 2006)

Allow students to use the following lists to figure out how they learn best. Some students may need to have the lists read to them.

Someone who is Verbal/Linguistic

- Tells tall tales, jokes, and stories
- Has a good memory
- Enjoys word games
- Enjoys reading and writing
- Has a good vocabulary for his/her age
- Has good verbal communication
- Enjoys crossword puzzles
- Appreciates nonsense rhymes, puns, tongue twisters, etc.
- Spells words accurately (or if preschool, spells using sounds that is advanced for age)

Someone who is Logical-Mathematical

- Asks questions about how things work
- Enjoys math activities
- Enjoys playing chess, checkers, or other strategy games
- Enjoys logic puzzles or brain teasers
- Interested in patterns, categories, and relationships
- Likes doing and creating experiments
- Does arithmetic problems in his or her head quickly (or if preschool, math concepts are advanced for age)
- Has a good sense of cause and effect

Someone who is Bodily Kinesthetic

- Excels in one or more sports or physical arts
- Moves, twitches, taps, or fidgets while seated for a long time
- Enjoys taking things apart and putting them back together
- Touches new objects
- Enjoys running, jumping, or wrestling
- Expresses him or herself dramatically
- Enjoys modeling clay and finger painting
- Good with his or her hands
- Cleverly mimics other people's gestures or mannerisms
- Reports different physical sensations while thinking or working

Someone who is Musical Rhythmic

- Recognizes off-key music
- Remembers melodies
- Plays a musical instrument or sings in a choir
- Speaks or moves rhythmically
- Taps rhythmically as he or she works
- Is sensitive to environmental noise
- Responds favorably to music
- Sings songs that he or she has learned outside of the classroom
- Is a discriminating listener
- Creates his or her own songs and melodies

Someone who is Intrapersonal

- Displays a sense of independence or a strong will
- Has a realistic sense of his or her strengths
- Has a good sense of self-direction
- Prefers working alone to working with others; may be shy
- Learns from his or her failures and successes
- Is insightful and self-aware
- Adapts well to his or her environment
- Aware of own emotions, strengths, and limitations
- Is self-disciplined
- Marches to the beat of different drummer in his/her style of living and learning

Someone who is Spatial

- Daydreams more than peers
- Enjoys art activities, puzzles, and mazes
- Likes visual presentations
- Understands more from pictures than words while reading
- Doodles on paper
- Loves construction sets: Legos, K'nex, Capsela, etc.
- Often inventing things
- Draws things that are advanced for age
- Reads maps, charts, and diagrams more easily than text (or if preschool, enjoys looking at more than text)

Someone who is Interpersonal

- Enjoys socializing with peers
- Acts as a natural leader
- Gives advice to friends who have problems
- Seems to be street-smart
- Belongs to clubs, committees, or other organizations
- Likes to play games with other kids
- Has one or more close friends
- Shows concern for others
- Perceives and makes distinctions in people's moods, intentions, and motivations
- Good at responding to other people's feelings

Someone who is Naturalist

- Enjoys labeling and identifying nature
- Sensitive to changes in weather
- Good at distinguishing among cars, sneakers, and jewelry, etc.

Someone Who Is Existentialist (Possible 9th Intelligence):

- Learns in the context of where humankind stands in the "big picture" of existence
- Asks "Why are we here?" and "What is our role in the world?"
- This intelligence is seen in the discipline of philosophy

Strategies: Multiple Intelligences & Differentiation

Suggestions for Assignments (Based on Multiple Intelligences)

For Verbal/Linguistic Learners

- ☐ Allow options for students to choose from when assigning projects, research, study, and practice
- ☐ Create radio or TV advertisements (see History Project example)
- ☐ Debate current events
- ☐ Create crossword puzzles
- ☐ Teach the class the steps to....
- ☐ Write a script

For Logical-Mathematical Learners

- ☐ Compare and contrast ideas
- ☐ Create a timeline
- ☐ Classify concepts/objects/materials
- ☐ Read or design maps
- ☐ Create a computer program
- ☐ Create story problems for....
- ☐ Design and conduct an experiment on....
- ☐ Use a Venn diagram to explain....
- ☐ Teach using technology

For Bodily Kinesthetic Learners

- ☐ Create hands-on projects
- ☐ Conduct hands-on experiments
- ☐ Create human sculptures to illustrate situations
- ☐ Design something that requires applying math concepts
- ☐ Re-enact great moments from history
- ☐ Study body language from different cultural situations
- ☐ Make task or puzzle cards for....

For Musical Rhythmic Learners

- ☐ Create "raps" (key dates, math, poems)
- ☐ Identify social issues through lyrics
- ☐ Analyze different historical periods through their music
- ☐ Make up sounds for different math operations or processes
- ☐ Use music to enhance the learning of....
- ☐ Write a new ending to a song so that it explains....

For Intrapersonal Learners

- ☐ Keep a journal to demonstrate learning
- ☐ Analyze historical personalities
- ☐ Imagine self as character in history, or scientist discovering a cure, or mathematician working a theory and describe or write about what you imagine to demonstrate learning

For Visual Spatial Learners

- ☐ Make visual organizer or memory model of the material being learned (give copies to other students in the class)
- ☐ Graph the results of a survey or results from a course of study
- ☐ Create posters or flyers
- ☐ Create collages
- ☐ Draw maps
- ☐ Study the art of a culture
- ☐ Color-code the process of....

For Interpersonal Learners

- ☐ Analyze a story
- ☐ Review material/concepts/books orally
- ☐ Discuss/debate controversial issues
- ☐ Find relationships between objects, cultures, situations
- ☐ Role-play a conversation with an important historical figure
- ☐ Solve complex word problems in a group
- ☐ Peer tutor the subject being learned

For Naturalist Learners

- ☐ Sort and classify content in relation to the natural world
- ☐ Interact with nature through field trips
- ☐ Encourage learning in natural surroundings
- ☐ Categorize facts about....

Theory: Brain-Based Research & Implications for Learning

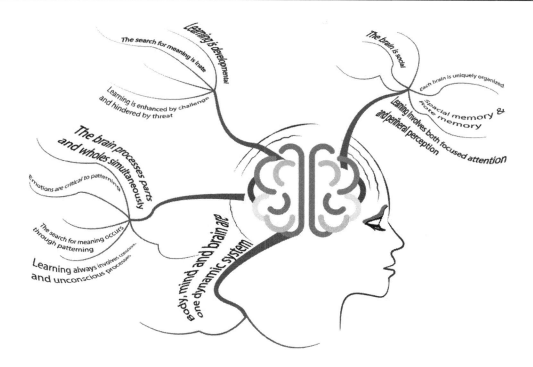

The search for meaning is innate

Learning is developmental

Learning is enhanced by challenge and hindered by threat

The brain processes parts and wholes simultaneously

Emotions are critical to patterning

The search for meaning occurs through patterning

Learning always involves conscious and unconscious processes

Body, mind and brain are one dynamic system

The brain is social

Each brain is uniquely organized

Spacial memory & rote memory

Learning involves both focused attention and peripheral perception

Questions and Answers About Brain Research

The brain reacts to shape, color, sound, texture, and light, yet teachers in the upper grades through high school still tend to teach through lecture — verbal linguistic methods. Focusing on language based teaching nourishes the left side of the brain but ignores the right side, which is dedicated to creative thinking.

Who Is Doing Brain Research?

Studies on the brain depend on research generated from the fields of Molecular Biology, psychoneuropharmacology, neurobiology, and neuroscience. The tools of exploration improve annually with advancements in computer technology and more precise methods of observing actual brain functioning as opposed to postmortem studies.

How Do Scientists Research the Brain?

Scientists use electrodes and amplifiers to map the brain's electrical activity. These studies are illuminating the sophisticated communication system established between brain cells. Neurobiologists study the communication between brain chemicals and the rest of the body's nervous system.

Neuroanatomists use electronic microscopes to trace the neural pathways from deep within the brain all the way down to the big toes.(Alivisatos et al., 2012; Kriegeskorte, Goebel, & Bandettini, 2006; Salmelin, Baillet, & Leahy, 2009)

Does Brain Research Prescribe Proven Methods of Instructions?

Neuroscience lends credibility to many principles of good instruction, but this field does not purport to prescribe specific ways to teach or a new and improved curriculum. Much of the work on the brain is applied from laboratory studies using mice, kittens, primates, fruit flies, samples of fetal tissue, and others. Educators must use caution when choosing teaching methods: don't throw the baby out with the bathwater (in comes brain-based techniques, out goes everything else, or vice versa). Yet there is significant evidence to warrant encouraging those charged with rearing and educating young children to carefully tend to the brain's intrinsic need for meaningful experience, nurturance, and safety.

12 Brain-Based Learning Principles

Renate Nummela Caine and Geoffrey Caine (Caine, Caine, McClintic, Klimek, & Costa, n.d.)identified basic patterns of how human beings learn. They call these the Twelve Principles of Brain-Based Learning.(Org, Caine, & Caine, n.d.) To summarize, there are at least twelve principles of brain-compatible learning that have emerged from brain research.

1. Uniqueness – Every single brain is totally unique and becomes more unique as we age.
2. A threatening environment or stress can alter and impair learning and even kill brain cells.
3. Emotions are critical to learning – They drive our attention, health, learning, meaning, and memory.
4. Information is stored and retrieved through multiple memory and neural pathways that are continually being formed.
5. All learning is mind-body – Movement, foods, attention cycles, drugs, and chemicals all have powerful modulating effects on learning.
6. The brain is a complex and adaptive system – Effective change involves the entire complex system.
7. Patterns and programs drive our understanding – Intelligence is the ability to elicit and to construct useful patterns.
8. The brain is meaning-driven – Meaning is more important to the brain than information.
9. Learning is often rich and non-conscious – We process both parts and wholes simultaneously and are affected a great deal by peripheral influences.
10. The brain develops better in concert with other brains – Intelligence is valued in the context of the society in which we live.
11. The brain develops with various stages of readiness.
12. Enrichment – The brain can grow new connections at any age. Complex, challenging experiences with feedback are best. Cognitive skills develop better with music and motor skills.

Strategies: Brain-Based Tips for the Classroom

☐ Dim the lights if possible, or use blue, green, pink, or full-spectrum lighting in the classroom (Cooper, 1999).

☐ Play classical music – Classical music connects with the brain, enabling students to learn better and to relax. Music should have less than 60 beats per minute.(Jausovec, Jausovec, & Gerlic, 2006) (Jausovec et al., 2006).

☐ Give students choices (Kohn, 1993).

☐ Use color to categorize, highlight important text, group like items, etc. (Hayes, Heit, & Rotello, 2014).

☐ Alternate the color of bullets on digital screens (eg. Interactive white boards), whiteboards, and chalkboards.

☐ Use colored borders for information that you want students to notice or remember.

☐ Border printed spelling words to accentuate the "shape" of the word.

☐ Allow opportunity for expressing emotions and listening to others' feelings.

☐ Take more stretch breaks and, when possible, incorporate brain-stimulating movement.

☐ Drink water – The brain needs hydration. Students need at least 40 ounces of water a day.

☐ Relate learning to real world experiences – Make it meaningful.

☐ Reduce stress in the classroom – Stress hinders learning. Students perform best when they do not feel they are competing with each other for the highest grades (Oei, Everaerd, Elzinga, van Well, & Bermond, 2006; Romain & Verdick, 2000; Vedhara, Hyde, Gilchrist, Tytherleigh, & Plummer, 2000).

☐ Use the "Power of Two" (work partners) for pulse learning.

☐ Use learner-imposed deadlines.

☐ Use graphic organizers, group and classify, and teach through telling stories!

☐ Create visual cues – draw pictures with stick figures or use clip art to illustrate important events and concepts. See Figures 1 and 2 by Sean McCready for examples.

Baron Friedrich Von Steuben

- Prussian army officer who served as a general in the American Revolution.
- Steuben served with Washington at Valley Forge
- At Valley Forge he trained the Americans to fight the British.

Von Steuben trained the Americans   to fight the British

Enlightenment

A movement in the 18th century where philosophers believed in man's ability to think

Enlightenment

Figure 1 & 2 courtesy of Sean McCready, Electronic Classrooms of Tomorrow, Ohio

Theory: Personality Preference and Learning Styles[1]

The Myers-Briggs Type Indicator® (MBTI®) reports a person's preferred way of 'being' in the world and his or her preferred process for making decisions.

Characteristics of Personality Types

- There are polar opposites for each preference, and each is useful and important
- Your preferences for certain mental habits are a persistent part of your personality
- There are no good or bad types
- Psychological type is not an intelligence test
- Everyone is an individual; type only helps us understand part of our personality (and learning style)
- The MBTI is an indicator, it indicates preference, it is not a test

Following is a description of the four scales reported in the MBTI and several teaching approaches that will appeal to different MBTI profiles.

Extraversion (E) Versus Introversion (I)

This preference tells us how people "get their energy."
- *Extraverts*[2] find energy in things and people. They prefer interaction with others, and are action-oriented. Extraverts are spontaneous thinkers who talk their thoughts aloud. Their motto is: Ready, Fire, Aim. For the extravert, there is no impression without expression.
- *Introverts* find energy in the inner world of ideas, concepts, and abstractions. They can be sociable, but need quiet to recharge their batteries. Introverts want to understand the world. Introverts concentrate and reflect. Their motto is: Ready, Aim, Aim... For the introvert, there is no impression without reflection.

---

[1] Information about Personality Preference and Learning style adapted from *The Master Teacher*, by Harvey J. Brightman, Georgia State University, and *Implications of Personality Type for Teaching and Learning* by John W. Pelley, Ph.D., Texas Tech University Health Sciences Center. (McKeachie, 1995; Sadler-Smith & Riding, 1999; Terregrossa, Englander, & Wang, 2010)

[2] The spelling of Extravert is derived from the works of Carl Jung and the Latin root meaning of extra.

> *"If you don't know what an extravert is thinking, you haven't been listening. But if you don't know what an introvert is thinking, you haven't asked!"*

Sensing (S) Versus Intuition (N)

This preference tells us how people take in information.

- *Sensing* types rely on their five senses. Sensing people are detail-oriented; they want facts and trust those facts.
- *Intuitive* types rely on their imagination and what can be seen in "the mind's eye." Intuitive people seek out patterns and relationships among the facts they have gathered. They trust hunches and their intuition and look for the "big picture."

> *"Sensing types help intuitives keep their heads out of the clouds,*
>
> *while intuitives help sensing types keep their heads out of a rut."*

Thinking (T) Versus Feeling (F)

This preference tells us how people make decisions.

- *Thinking* types prefer to decide things impersonally based on analysis, logic, and principle. Thinking students value fairness. What could be fairer than focusing on the situation's logic, and placing great weight on objective criteria in making a decision?
- *Feeling* types prefer to make decisions by focusing on human values. Feeling students value harmony. They focus on human values and needs as they make decisions or arrive at judgments. They tend to be good at persuasion and easing differences among group members.

> *"Thinking types need to remember that feelings are also facts they need to consider, while feeling types need to remember that thinking types have feelings too!"*

Judging (J) Versus Perceptive (P)

This preference tells us people's attitudes toward the outside world.

- *Judging* types prefer to make quick decisions. Judging people are decisive, planful (they make plans), and self-regimented. They focus on completing the task, only want to know the essentials, and take action quickly (perhaps too quickly). They plan their work and work their plan. Deadlines are sacred. Their motto is: Just do it!
- *Perceptive* types prefer to postpone action and seek more data. Perceptive people are curious, adaptable, and spontaneous. They start many tasks, want to know everything about each task, and often find it difficult to complete a task. Deadlines are meant to be stretched. Their motto is: On the other hand...

> *"Judging types can help perceiving types meet deadlines, while perceiving types can help keep judging types open to new information."*

Additional Resources:

- The MBTI instrument is available from Consulting Psychological Press in Palo Alto, California.
- Works by David Ausubel (Ausubel, 1963).

Information about Personality Preference and Learning Style is adapted from *The Master Teacher*, by Harvey J. Brightman, Georgia Satte University, and *Implications of Personality Type for Teaching and Learning* by John W. Peltey, Ph.D., Texas Tech University Health Science Center. (Article, 2004, Sadler-Smith & Riding, 1999; Terregrassa, Englander, & Wang, 2010)

Strategies: Personality Preference/Learning Style

Strategies for Teaching Introverted Students

Introverted students want to develop frameworks that integrate or connect the subject matter. To an introvert, disconnected chunks are not knowledge; rather, they are merely information. Knowledge means interconnecting material and seeing the "big picture."

To engage introverts:
- ☐ Provide written materials ahead of time – especially if you want discussion or decisions immediately
- ☐ Pause when asking for response – 20 seconds is effective (but hard for extraverts)
- ☐ Be prepared to draw out some individuals with specific questions
- ☐ Teach students how to chunk, or group and interconnect, knowledge. Introverted students will appreciate it, although extraverted students may not. Nevertheless, cognitive psychologists tell us that through chunking, students master the material. It is also suggested that students learn to build a compare/contrast table, flowchart, or concept map when learning new material

Strategies for Teaching Extraverted Students

Extraverted students learn by explaining to others. They do not know if they understand the subject until they try to explain it to themselves or others. Extraverted students often say that they thought they knew the material until they tried to explain it to a fellow student. Only then did they realize they did not understand the subject.

To engage extraverts
- ☐ Convey energy and enthusiasm about the topic
- ☐ Allow time for participation and discussion

Extraverted students enjoy working in groups. Consider in-class or outside-of-class group exercises and projects.

Some suggested activities:
- ☐ Thinking Aloud Paired Problem Solving (TAPPS) method
- ☐ Think-Pair-Share
- ☐ Teaching Each Other
- ☐ Peer Practice Activity
- ☐ Jigsaw

These methods support learning through explaining but provide quiet time for introverted students.

Inter and Intrapersonal learners, Verbal Linguistics, incorporating brain-based research and fostering long-term retention of course content.

TAPPS

1. Teacher poses question and provides quiet time for students.
2. Teacher designates the explainer and listener within each pair.
3. Explainers explain ideas to listeners. Listeners can (1) ask questions for clarification, (2) disagree, or (3) provide hints when explainers become lost.
4. Teacher critiques some explainers' answers and provides closure.

Think/Pair/Share

Think/Pair/Share (Gregory & Kuzmich, 2007) is a strategy designed to provide students with "food for thought" on a given topic. This enables students to formulate their own ideas and share them with another student.

1. Teacher poses a question to the class/group.
2. Teacher gives students one to two minutes to think about the questions and make some personal connections.
3. Teacher instructs the students to form pairs and share their thinking with each other.

OPTIONS:
- Students form new pairs and share again.
- After think/pair/share, class as a whole joins in discussion.

Teaching Each Other

(O'Donnell King, Alison et al., 1999)

1. Students are pre-arranged in pairs.
2. Assign partner A and partner B.
3. Teach ten minutes – stop.
4. Set time for one to two minutes.
5. Partner A teaches Partner B one thing you've taught them in the past ten minutes.
6. Set timer for one to two minutes.
7. Class shares what they learned.
8. Repeat for one more round.

Peer Practice Activity

PEER PRACTICE IN ASTRONOMY	
TASK B QUESTIONS	**TASK A ANSWERS**
UNIVERSE	A hot, glowing globe of gas that emits energy
SUPERCLUSTER	The sun and its collection of 9 planets
LOCAL GROUP	An object that revolves around a star
GALAXY (Milky Way)	Study of everything beyond the earth
SUN'S NEIGHBORS	Groupings of stars based upon the imagination of man

PEER PRACTICE IN ASTRONOMY	
TASK A QUESTIONS	**TASK B ANSWERS**
STAR (Sun)	All of space and what is found in it
SOLAR SYSTEM	A collection of galaxies, which include the local group
PLANET (Earth)	The Milky Way and its twenty closest neighbors
ASTRONOMY	A vast collection of stars, gas, and dust
CONSTELLATION	The sun and its twenty closest neighbors

Instructions
1. Create practice sheets as above with the QUESTIONS (in short hand) on one side and answers to those QUESTIONS on the other side of the Partner sheet and vice versa.
2. Have students fold the sheets down the middle so that they are looking at only questions or answers.
3. For example, one partner looks at TASK A questions and the other partner looks at TASK B answers.
4. Students quiz each other by mixing up the order they ask the questions or cue with the answers.

Keep Questions and answers to five to seven chunks of information on one sheet.

Save yourself some work: Have students create their own practice sheets, then photocopy for the class.

Jigsaw

Jigsaw (Aronson, Elliot; Patnoe, 1997) is a cooperative learning strategy that incorporates the most effective method of learning according to brain-based research: I learn when I teach it. Students meet with members of other groups who are assigned the same topic, and after mastering the material, return to the original group and teach the material to the original group members.

1. Divide students into groups of four.
2. Assign a topic or section of material to each group member.
3. Each student finds other students with the same topic or section and forms a new group of "experts".
4. This new group learns together, becoming experts on their topic.
5. Once students are comfortable with the material, they rejoin their original group.
6. Student topic experts teach their original group the subject matter.

**Several short jigsaw events with manageable chunks of subject matter might be more effective than assigning large amounts of material.

A Visual Representation of How Jigsaw Works

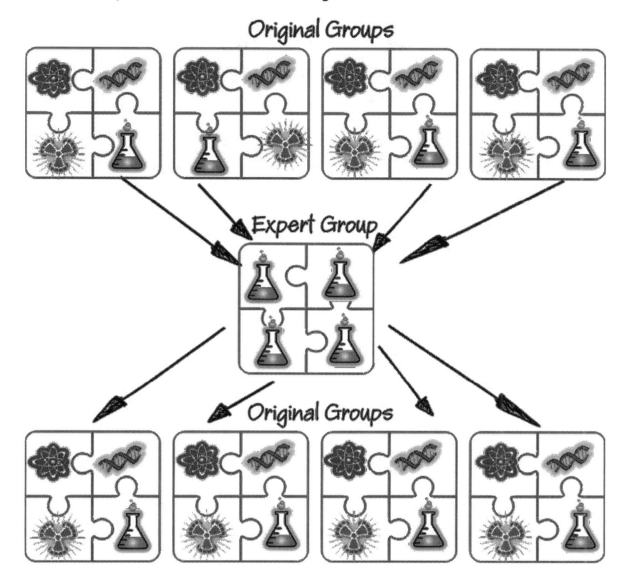

JIGSAW OPTION
1. Students in a group are each given a different paragraph from a reading selection, or different paragraphs offering different views of the same subject.
2. Students read their paragraph silently.
3. Students then explain what they read to the rest of the group.
4. (This option requires confident readers.)

Strategies for Teaching Sensing Types

Visual Spatial Learners, Incorporating Brain-based Research

Sensing students prefer organized, linear, and structured lessons. Sensing preferences tend to produce linear learners. They tend to test worse than their actual knowledge, and tend to apply better than their actual knowledge.

When presenting lessons include specifics, facts, and details, show why it is realistic and makes sense. Include real life applications and examples of where this has worked before.

Three suggested methods for organizing a lecture:
- ☐ What Must Be Known (WMBK) method
- ☐ KWHL Method
- ☐ The Application-Theory-Application (A-T-A) method
- ☐ Advanced organizers

WMBK Activity (Daniels, 2000)

1. Ask: What is (are) the topic's most essential general principle(s) or goals?
2. Place the answer in a goal box.
3. Ask: What topic(s) do the students need to know in order to achieve the goal?
4. Place these sub-goal boxes below the goal box and show an arrow leading from each sub-goal box to the goal box.
5. Continue to ask WMBK questions until you connect with material previously covered. Present new subject material by starting at the bottom of the diagram and work up toward the goal box.

Goal: What Must Be Learned?

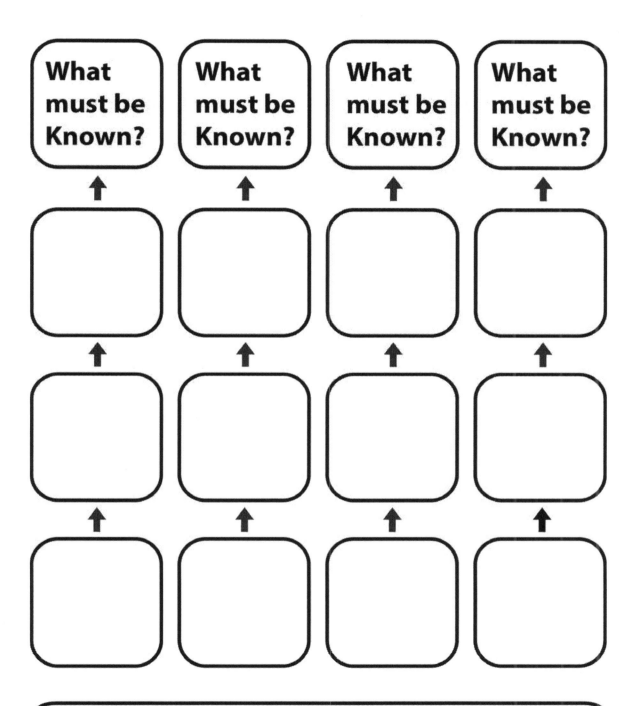

What must be Known?	What must be Known?	What must be Known?	What must be Known?

What must be known for students to be able to achieve the goal?

KWHL Method

K-W-L (Ogle, 1986)is an instructional strategy that can be used when reading in English/Language Arts, or in the content area. It is used to guide students through a text. The H for "How I will learn it" is an option that aligns with the goals of Personalized Learning.

Students:

1. Start by brainstorming everything they Know about the topic they will be reading about.
2. Then, students record the information in the K column of a K-W-L chart.
3. Students then generate a list of questions about what they Want to Know about the topic, or what they want to solve (e.g. math or science). These questions are listed in the W column of the chart.
4. Some teachers add the H column to help students to take ownership of their learning. Here, they list ways they will be an active participant in their learning. How will they learn it. Encourage them to consider their learning style when planning the "How".
5. During or after reading, students write down what they learned in response to the questions in the "W" column. This new information that they have Learned is recorded in the L column of the K-W-L chart.

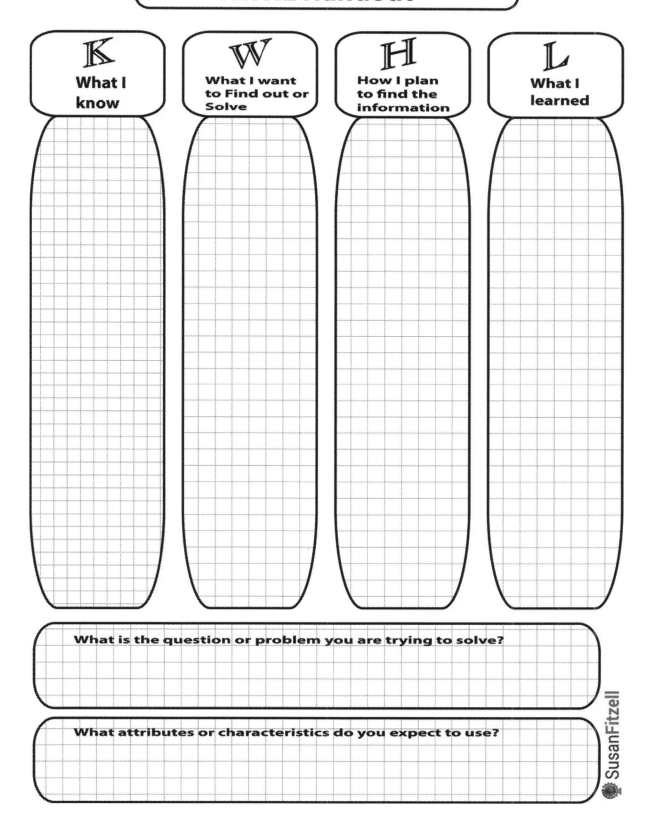

KWHL Handout

K What I know	**W** What I want to Find out or Solve	**H** How I plan to find the information	**L** What I learned

What is the question or problem you are trying to solve?

What attributes or characteristics do you expect to use?

SusanFitzell

Application-Theory-Application (A-T-A) Method

1. Present a problem or mini-case (Application) to the class.
2. Students attempt to analyze and solve the case or problem **without** the benefit of the upcoming chapter's theory or ideas.
3. The problem or mini-case *motivates* sensing students to learn the material.
4. Mini-case studies, (Applications) answer the question that sensing students often ask: "Why am I learning this material?"
5. After the class has struggled with the problem (and sometimes emerged victoriously), present the chapter's (T)heory or ideas, and then apply it to the original application.
6. Afterwards, present additional (A)pplications and have the students apply the theory.

An opening application problem or mini-case should
- be familiar to students
- engage their curiosity
- be **almost** solvable from previous text material or student experiences, and
- be baffling, or counter-intuitive, if possible

A familiar problem assures sensing students that their experiences have prepared them to address the problem. Being "almost solvable" minimizes students' frustrations. The application should be "just beyond a student's reach." However, previously learned material or experiences should help students make a reasonable solution attempt. An application that is too significant a leap will cause frustration and the feeling that the teacher is playing games with the students.

Advanced Organizers As Defined by David Ausubel

1. The most general ideas of a subject should be presented first and then progressively differentiated in terms of detail and specifics.
2. Instructional materials should attempt to integrate new material with previously presented information through comparisons and cross-referencing of new and old ideas.

Develop advanced organizers by answering the following questions:
- What do students know that at a very general level is similar to the subject matter about to be taught?
- How can I demonstrate the connections between what is known and what is to be learned (Ausubel, 1963)?

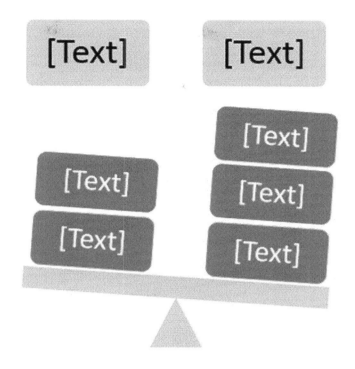

Sample Advanced Organizers

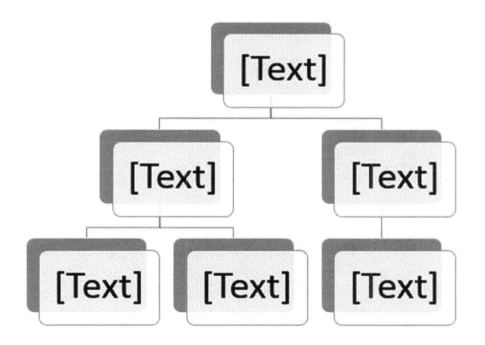

Provide a Syllabus

A syllabus provides the structure that supports how a sensing type (a student who needs the details laid out) learns.

NAME_____

World History/Textbook Assignments

Follow each set of directions below for work in the textbook. Also, pay attention to the due dates as listed. These will be graded assignments. Many are "thought" questions, so be careful to read and answer what is being asked.

Due Friday, May 5

Chapter 21
Use the chapter to help you do the following assignments on pages 686–687.
    ☐ **Using Key Terms: Do questions #1-17**
    ☐ **Reviewing the Facts: Do questions #5, 7, and 8**

Due Monday, May 8

    Chapter 22
    ☐ **Read page 688**
    ☐ **Read page 691**   ☐ **Answer question #3**
    ☐ **Read page 694**   ☐ **Answer question #2**
    ☐ **Read page 702–703**   ☐ **Answer question #4**
    ☐ **Read page 704–705**   ☐ **Answer question #3**
    ☐ **Read page 706–707**   ☐ **Answer question #2**
    ☐ **Read page 719–720**

Due Tuesday, May 9, 2010

Chapter 22, continued

Use the chapter to help you do the following assignments on pages 726–727
    ☐ **Reviewing the Facts: Do questions #2, 5, 7, 9, 13**
    ☐ **Thinking Critically: Do questions #1, 9**

Due Wednesday, May 10
    Use chapters 23 and 24 to gain a definition and understanding of the following terms: COLONIALISM and IMPERIALISM

Contributed by Barbara Mee, Social Studies Teacher, Londonderry High School

Strategies for Teaching Intuitive Types

Interpersonal learners, incorporating brain-based research and fostering long-term retention of course content, also for Logical-Mathematical, Verbal Linguistic. Use mind maps and add Visual Spatial.

The small group discovery method will appeal to intuitive students and will teach sensing students how to uncover general principles. In using this method, sensing and intuitive students should be combined in learning groups. The intuitive student can help the sensing student discover the theory; the sensing student can help identify and marshal the facts of the exercise.

Intuitive students must have the big picture, or an integrating framework, to understand a subject. The big picture shows how the subject matter is interrelated. Intuitive students can develop reasonably correct concept maps or compare and contrast tables. Fortunately, sensing students can be taught to do the same.

- ☐ Give intuitives an overview of the day's lesson(s) at the beginning
- ☐ Put new information in context
- ☐ Mention several possibilities; review alternatives
- ☐ Talk about innovative happenings and current events

Small Group Discovery Method

Neil Davidson(Davidson, 1971) developed the small group discovery method in 1967 at the University of Wisconsin. He started with the idea established by R.L. Moore that bright students can develop mathematics. He then changed the social environment to render the idea workable for much larger numbers of students in undergraduate courses.

The discovery method concept can be successful for math problems, science case studies, social studies "investigations" or mysteries, and alternative solutions for conflicts in literature.

1. Divide the class into small groups of three to four students.
2. Each group discusses the problem to be solved (theorem) and proves it cooperatively as a group effort during class.
3. Every group has its own section of the board for working space.
4. Members write a group solution on the board for each problem.
5. Teacher moves from group to group, checking solutions (proofs) on the board and giving suggestions for improvement, asking probing questions to help guide, or giving hints.
6. Design problems that can be solved in one class period.

Advantage: A group of students will solve a problem that each of the group members would give up on if he or she was working on it by himself or herself.

Overview Method

This one is simple, yet, critical: Start with an overview of the topic.

Strategies for Teaching Thinking Students

Thinking students like clear course and topic objectives. Clear course or topic objectives avoid vague words or expressions such as "students will appreciate" or "be exposed to." Rather, objectives need to be precise and action-oriented. Precise objectives clearly define the type of learning that will happen: rote, meaningful and integrated, or critical thinking. In action-oriented objectives, the verbs describe what students must do, not what teachers will do. Bloom's taxonomy provides guidelines for writing clear and meaningful objectives.

- ☐ List all the pros and cons, when possible, in the lesson.
- ☐ Structure the class material logically.
- ☐ Be succinct – Teachers who ramble lose thinking students.
- ☐ Define clear objectives.
- ☐ Have action-oriented lessons.
- ☐ List pros and cons as related to your topic.
- ☐ Don't ramble or go off on tangents, it drives thinking types crazy or you lose them.
- ☐ Structure class material logically.

Strategies for Teaching Feeling Students

Feeling students like working in groups, especially harmonious groups. They enjoy the small group exercises such as TAPPS and the Nominal Group Method. To promote harmonious groups, provide students with guidelines on how to work best in a group.

- ☐ Be friendly and collaborative.
- ☐ Show how the subject of the lesson impacts people – especially why it is important to the individuals involved.
- ☐ Express appreciation for student contributions.
- ☐ Provide opportunity for interaction. (See Strategies for Introverts and Extraverts.)
- ☐ Place importance on class harmony.
- ☐ Be friendly and collaborative.
- ☐ Show the impact of whatever you are teaching has on people, especially why it is important to the individuals involved.
- ☐ Express appreciation for student contributions.

Strategies for Teaching Judging Types

We have found that the following hints on note taking and test taking help judging students learn more effectively:

- ☐ Speedwriting
- ☐ Split Page
- ☐ Color Coding
- ☐ AOR Model
- ☐ Reverse Question
- ☐ Treating Objective Questions as Essay Question
- ☐ Remind Judging types to check their answers and take a second look when solving problems.

Judging students often reach too quickly for closure when analyzing cases.

Speedwriting

Most students can learn speedwriting in several minutes. Just omit all (or most) vowels. Or develop your own shorthand method. For example, <u>mst stdnts cn lrn spdwrtng in svrl mnts. Jst omt ll or mst vwls.</u>

Split Pages

Draw a line down the center of a notebook page. On the left hand side, record the lecture (use speedwriting or your own shorthand notation). After class, write a **commentary** on the right-hand side. Include restating ideas in your own words, finding sources of confusion, identifying key points, looking for links to earlier learned material, and asking "What does this mean to me? (The student)."

Color Coding

Use different colors to record ideas presented in class and found in the text or readings. For example, use blue to code major ideas and green to code links to previously learned material.(Ozcelik, Karakus, Kursun, & Cagiltay, 2009; Wong, 2010)

AOR Model

In answering an essay question, first Analyze the question and jot down key ideas, Organize the ideas into a logical sequence, and only then write the essay (Respond).

Reverse Question

To review an essay question, first read your answer. Then construct an essay question based on your answer. Now compare your question to the teacher's question. If different, revise your answer. This strategy ensures that students answer the teacher's question.

Treat Objective Questions as Essay Questions

Read the question's stem (the portion that contains the question) and write a brief answer. Then compare your answer to the four or five choices, and select the answer most similar to your mini-essay.

Strategies for Teaching Perceiving Types

Perceptive students often postpone doing an assignment until the very last minute. They are not lazy. Quite the contrary; they seek information to the very last minute (and sometimes beyond).

- ☐ Break assignments down into chunks with parts due at specific dates that lead up to the final due date. These deadlines will help to keep the perceptive types on target. It also allows you to give ongoing feedback to the student, adding to the final quality of the assignment.
- ☐ Help students set goals.
- ☐ Use audio files to give frequent feedback.*
- ☐ Teach them to use organizers.
- ☐ Break down assignments.
- ☐ Help students set goals.
- ☐ Teach them to use organizers.
- ☐ Use voice recorder apps to give frequent feedback.
- ☐ Use Voice recorder apps for Feedback on Assignments.
- ☐ Instruct students to email voice memos with their sub-assignments.
- ☐ While reading the assignment, make comments on the voice memo (we speak faster than we can write) on content and grammar.

*Teachers who have used the audio feedback approach found final papers were clearer and more readable, and thus less aggravation to read. In addition, it affords students an opportunity to improve their writing skills during the semester because of the 'verbal' feedback at different stages of completion of the assignment.

General Type Considerations for Teachers

- ☐ Extraverts need dialogue.
- ☐ Introverts need time to think.
- ☐ Intuitives are way ahead of you.
- ☐ Sensing types and judging types need a sense of structure in the instruction; uncertainty about organization of lesson will discourage learning.
- ☐ Feeling types need human contact; failure to communicate on a personal level will discourage learning.
- ☐ Thinking types need answers to questions that make sense; learning is business, not personal.
- ☐ Stop at frequent intervals and ask for questions. Asking students by name for questions will help to involve the introverts.
- ☐ Make frequent reference to a lesson outline. Point out when digression from outline begins and when it ends.
- ☐ Point out, as questions are asked in class, how it has helped in contributing to the lesson. This makes feeling types feel very valuable.

☐ Use the reflection method to rephrase questions. This will help clarify for sensing types what is being asked.

☐ Develop collaborative learning exercises that require the use of concepts taught.

Information about Personality Preference and Learning style was adapted from *The Master Teacher*, by Harvey J. Brightman, Georgia State University, and *Implications of Personality Type for Teaching and Learning* by John W. Pelley, Ph.D., Texas Tech University Health Sciences Center, and the Myers-Briggs Type Indicator description pamphlets.

Thought Provoking Quotes: Personality & Learning Style

I may be your spouse, your parent, your offspring, your friend, or your colleague. If you will allow me any of my own wants, or emotions, or beliefs, or actions, then you open yourself, so that someday these ways of mine might not seem so wrong, and might finally appear to you as right – for me. To put up with me is the first step to understanding me. Not that you embrace my ways as right for you, but that you are no longer irritated or disappointed with me for my seeming waywardness. And in understanding me you might come to prize my differences from you, and, far from seeking to change me, preserve and even nurture those differences.

--Please Understand Me II by David Keirsey

The most essential thing to know about the motivations of types is that thinking dominant types do their best work when pursuing logical order; feeling types do their best work when their heart is in it; sensing types do their best work when their practical skills are needed and valued; and intuitive types do their best work when pursuing an inspiration.

--People Types and Tiger Stripes Third Edition by Gordon Lawrence

Chapter 1 Review & Discussion Questions

Differentiated Instruction

1. After reading this section of the chapter, do you feel that you differentiate your lessons?
2. If yes, what methods of presentation, practice, and evaluation do you routinely use?
3. If no, where do you think you should start to adjust your lessons to provide differentiated instruction?
4. How might you use the lesson components and steps for planning in the chapter to meet student needs and ensure that you are consistently planning to incorporate multiple strategies that accommodate all levels of learners and learning styles in your classroom?

Multiple Intelligences

1. After reading the section and using the tools and techniques offered, how many different "intelligences" can you identify in the students you are currently teaching?
2. Do you feel that your current teaching practices are appropriate and meaningful for each of your students and their primary "intelligence?" Why, or why not?
3. What is the relationship between the methods used in lesson presentation and student success?

Brain-Based Learning Techniques

1. After reviewing the twelve brain-based learning principles, how many of these principles do you consciously acknowledge and employ in your day-to-day teaching?
2. Which, if any, of the brain-based tips for your classroom are you currently using?
3. Identify two brain-based tips that you might work to incorporate into your teaching immediately.

Personality Preference and Learning Styles

1. Based only on your observations in your classroom, and using the information in this section, approximately how many different learning styles do you deal with on a daily basis?
2. What questions might you ask when talking with students to informally assess their learning style? How might you make use of that information to guide instruction?

Practical Application

- Create a three column chart.
- List the activities presented in this section to address various learning styles and personality types in the first column.
- After you have created a list, identify which of these activities require higher-order thinking, or problem solving, or connection to real world learning, or active learning, and list them in the second column.
- Analyze the data in the first two columns and devise a simple plan for mixing these strategies into one week of lessons so that all levels of Blooms Taxonomy or Depth of Knowledge are addressed, and all learners are presented with some amount of information in their learning style.
- Keep it simple. The goal is to think about how you might incorporate a variety of strategies, over the period of a week, to ensure that we are reaching all learners and incorporating multiple levels of thinking skills during your lessons.

Group Brainstorm

Brainstorm ideas for student engagement and active learning based on your understanding of how "different learners learn differently".

Challenge Question

The call for rigor in our curriculum content, and expectations is dominating educational discussions across the nation. What is rigor? Can we differentiate instruction and still embrace educational rigor?

✂ **CHAPTER 2** ✂

Collaboration & Co-teaching

Gangs in the Classroom

Back in 2003, I was working in classrooms coaching co-teachers at a high school in a tough part of town. I walked into this one room with nothing more than a list of room numbers and teacher names. I didn't know which teacher was the special education teacher or which one was the English teacher. I had been warned by the administration that it was a very apathetic group of students in that particular class.

There were two teachers in the front of the room, and I couldn't tell who was who because they were both up front leading a lively discussion about a piece of literature the class was reading.

All the students were engaged. What really struck me was people were disagreeing with each other; including the two teachers. They were discussing the author's intent, debating his motivation, characterization, and purpose intensely. The two teachers took opposing views. Students were passionately sharing their perspectives. I was enthralled. This is apathy? No! It's prodigious.

At the end of the day, in our debriefing session, I asked, "How did you get to the point where you could work seamlessly together to engage students in such an energetic debate? It's clear that you two click and work well together."

They replied, "We've worked at it." "But you know what, if you visited our classroom in September you wouldn't have seen this. We couldn't even put our students in pairs at the beginning of the school year to do a think-pair-share because we have four gangs represented in this classroom.

At the beginning of the semester, we made the mistake of putting two gang members from opposing gangs together and had a fist fight break out in the room! We quickly realized we couldn't sit certain students together so we just didn't. When we tried to have a class debate and include the students, if one gang member disagreed with an opposing gang member, they were literally climbing over desks to confront each other nose-to-nose. This was a problem."

The teachers explained that they couldn't involve students in discussion that provoked critical thinking skills until students could discuss an issue without feeling that any disagreement was a sign of disrespect for their gang.

Their solution:

Model respectful debate for the students all semester.

They demonstrated that just because you disagree with someone doesn't mean that's a cause to fight. Disagreement doesn't mean disrespect. People have a right to their own opinion.

Upon reflection of our debriefing session, I realized that it was the first time I had been exposed to the idea that co- teaching is a wonderful means for students to learn respectful collaboration and debate.

Colleagues of mine, Kathy and Peter, taught social studies together and loved to enliven the classroom with theatrics. They decided to role-play different sides of a political issue to accentuate the different standpoints on two sides of an election debate.

They set the stage:

Kathy stood on one side of the door and Peter stood on the other. As students entered through the doorway to class they had to walk between two teachers who were debating a political issue taking opposite stands. They feigned intensity and passion in their disagreement.

The bell rang and the students sat in their seats waiting for class to begin (and for the teachers to calm down.) Instead, Kathy and Peter followed the students into the room and took it up a level. They got a little bit louder and then they started pulling the students into the debate. "Trish, what do you think? What do you think about this issue? Do you agree with...?"

They made it personal but refrained from becoming disrespectful or antagonistic. They were successful in engaging their class in thoughtful discussion.

The brain loves and learns through emotion. They had the emotion and the energy to draw students; and the loud factor.

What a wonderful way to convey two stances on an issue! It's really difficult to do that all by yourself, so modeling disagreement and debate is a powerful benefit to co-teaching done well!

Collaboration Approaches

Collaborative Roles in the Classroom

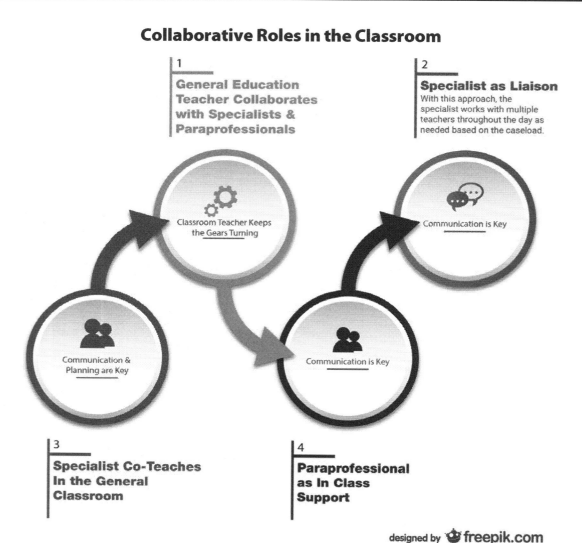

1

General Education Teacher Collaborates with Specialists & Paraprofessionals

2

Specialist as Liaison
With this approach, the specialist works with multiple teachers throughout the day as needed based on the caseload.

Classroom Teacher Keeps the Gears Turning

Communication is Key

Communication & Planning are Key

Communication is Key

3

Specialist Co-Teaches in the General Classroom

4

Paraprofessional as In Class Support

designed by freepik.com

General Education

Given the magnitude of demands placed on classroom teachers today, they can become overwhelmed with the task of trying to meet the needs of a heterogeneously grouped co-taught classroom. Whereas some content area teachers are skilled in working with students with disabilities, and some may even have certification in special education, we cannot assume a general education teacher has that knowledge and background. Even when a teacher "can" meet the demands of today's' rigorous standards as well as the needs of their students, the opportunity to collaborate with specialists to meet student needs significantly increases the level of student success.

Specialist as Liaison

At times, the specialist acts as 'consultant' to the general classroom teacher. The special education 'consultant' works primarily outside the classroom with the general education teacher and may work directly in classrooms as needed. The general classroom teacher in this situation makes most, if not all, of the classroom adaptations, accommodations, and modifications, using the IEP and the special educator as a guide and resource.

Specialist Co-teaches in the General Classroom

Special education teachers can play a critical role in helping classroom and content area teachers analyze the standards-based lesson plan and design lessons that support all learners in the classroom. State Standards place new demands on content area teachers as well as special education teachers. It's important that both teachers take an active role in professional development that enables the special education teacher to become skilled in the content, as well as enabling the general education teacher to understand how to differentiate lesson plans and deliver **Specially Designed Instruction (SDI)** when necessary.

Paraprofessional as in-Class Support

If a paraprofessional is assigned to the general classroom, the special education teacher or specialist works closely with both the paraprofessional and the general classroom teacher.

Collaboration Approaches[3]

One Teacher, One Support Teacher • Subject expert often lead teacher • Support teacher often specialist	Support teacher's role defined by IEPs. The more time spent planning and collaborating, the more benefit to all in the classroom.
Parallel Teaching • Divide the class in half • Both teach the same content to smaller group • Plan together for consistency	It's important to not be hierarchical and to divide the student mix carefully so that both groups have a variety of students that work well together.
Alternative Teaching • Usually one large group & one smaller group • May teach the same or different content • Each teach their content, then switch • Allows teachers to use their individual strengths while teaching	This is a good approach to use as needed. Having several small groups for different purposes would also eliminate some of the stigma of the student with learning disabilities always being singled out.
Teach Half then Switch • Divide the class in half • Both teach DIFFERENT content to smaller group • Plan together for consistency	It's important to not be hierarchical and to divide the student mix carefully so that both groups have a variety of students that work well together.
Acceleration Centers® • Shared instruction and planning • Coordinated activities and dialog • Provides great flexibility	This approach is one of the most effective formats for addressing a wide range of abilities in the general education classroom.
Station Teaching • Shared instruction and planning • Coordinated activities and dialog • Provides great flexibility	With Station teaching, students move from one station to the next, within a specific chunk of time to complete targeted activities.
Flexible Grouping • Shared instruction and planning • Coordinated activities and dialog • Provides great flexibility	Essentially, flexible grouping is the process of grouping and re-grouping based on content, interest, learning style, or data.
Team Teaching • Shared instruction and planning • Coordinated activities and dialog • Trust, commitment, and personality compatibility a must	Many see this situation as the ideal; however, it requires two teachers who are compatible in personality style, commitment, and teaching philosophy, who are also given the time and support to plan together.

---

[3] Adapted from the original Co-teaching models of Dr. Marilyn Friend (Friend, 2014a)

Paraprofessionals in the Classroom

A Paraprofessional's Point of View

Teamwork between the paraprofessional and the classroom teacher is an essential ingredient to a successful inclusion classroom. When a paraprofessional is assigned to a class, he or she should be seen as a part of the solution and not as an intrusion.

Ideally, the paraprofessional and the classroom teacher have some common planning time to discuss upcoming assignments, progress of students, and methods to help the students succeed. Without this time, it is difficult to establish a strong working relationship; however, the relationship can still be beneficial.

Paraprofessionals can be valuable resources in the classroom. They can work in class with students who are having difficulty understanding the information, provide notes for those students who are unable to take comprehensive notes during class time, and provide help with test and assignment modifications for students with learning disabilities.

Student follow-up is especially important to meet IEP requirements and promote success. Often, the paraprofessional can follow-up in the resource room as well as in-class. Paraprofessionals can support the classroom teacher by answering the questions of all students.

Paraprofessionals are an integral and important part of the classroom team. They are happy to contribute whatever they can to add to the success of all the students. If the teacher is accepting of the paraprofessional's presence, then the students will also accept it as normal and will consider him or her as the extra, valuable resource he or she is.

Ginger Davis
Londonderry High School

Communication and an Organized Approach

One of the most important aspects of an effective working relationship between the paraprofessional, special educator, teacher, or specialist is clear and consistent communication and organization. It is critical to communicate frequently and use organizing tools that can help define roles, define expectations, and set parameters for class norms as part of the communication process. Why is structure and time to talk so important? Because without having a system in place to discuss issues, organize information, and handle variables, much is subject to guesswork, and guesswork often causes problems and communication breakdown.

A paraprofessional often enters the classroom with a tremendous amount of concern about intruding on the teacher's space. Many times, this concern can lead to inaction, a lesser quality of experience for both the paraeducator and teacher, and sometimes can even lead to feelings of intimidation. Time spent communicating - establishing rapport, documenting, and organizing roles, expectations, and schedules - can make the difference between a harmonious relationship and one filled with discord.

It is important for both teachers and paraeducators to understand that a paraprofessional's job is demanding and varies tremendously from one class to the other. He may not know what he will encounter in any one situation, what he will be required to do once he walks in that classroom door, or what personalities he may have to navigate.

One of the trickiest parts of working in the classroom as a paraprofessional is understanding the paraprofessional's role. What is that role? Each student's needs determine the paraprofessional's role, whether they are academic needs or behavioral needs, and often these are dictated by the IEP or the special education department. Sometime,s a paraprofessional is working with one single student. Other times, a paraprofessional may be working with an entire class of students. In that situation, the paraprofessional may be working as a classroom assistant because many students in the classroom are on an IEP.

It is very difficult in these situations to walk into a classroom without any prior dialogue as to what the paraprofessional's roles and responsibilities will include. The paraprofessional's job is to support and assist students within the classroom using the IEPs of the student, or several students, involved to provide the framework. The supervising special or general education teacher is responsible for direct instruction, providing assistance, and guiding the paraprofessional to work effectively with individual students. It is important that the paraprofessional feels positive about the work he or she is doing and feels in harmony with the classroom teacher.(Giangreco, Edelman, & Broer, 2001)

Defining the Role of the

Paraprofessional

Least Effective Use of Paraeducators' Skills(Brock & Carter, 2013; McVay, 1998):

The general education teacher and students both lose a valuable resource if the paraprofessional's role is to:

- Photocopy papers
- Copy notes (solely)
- Run errands
- Hold up the back wall of the classroom, figuratively speaking.

Ways Paraprofessionals Support

Inclusive Classrooms

The ways a paraprofessional might assist in the classroom are as individual as the students they are responsible for, the classrooms they work in, and the grade level they teach.

On the following pages are checklists filled with options for the general education teacher, the special education teacher, and the paraprofessional to consider when defining paraprofessional roles in the classroom.

Use these checklists as a tool to negotiate the working relationship in the classroom before the paraprofessional starts "on the job."

Checklists excerpted from *Paraprofessionals and Teachers Working Together* by Susan Fitzell (S. Fitzell, 2010)

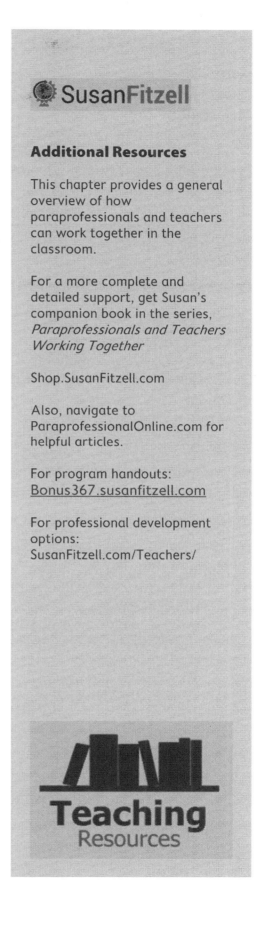

SusanFitzell

Additional Resources

This chapter provides a general overview of how paraprofessionals and teachers can work together in the classroom.

For a more complete and detailed support, get Susan's companion book in the series, *Paraprofessionals and Teachers Working Together*

Shop.SusanFitzell.com

Also, navigate to ParaprofessionalOnline.com for helpful articles.

For program handouts:
Bonus367.susanfitzell.com

For professional development options:
SusanFitzell.com/Teachers/

Teaching Resources

One-to-One Assistant

Classroom Teacher:

Subject:

Student Initials:

- ☐ Support student in getting ready for in-class assignments or for other activities so he or she can keep up with the class while at the same time learning how to become more independent.
- ☐ Substitute activities without changing curriculum.
- ☐ Adapt instructional materials in accordance with the IEP.
- ☐ Re-teach instruction and provide reinforcement.
- ☐ Assist the student with individual activities.
- ☐ Help student with makeup work.
- ☐ Assist student with interpreting and following directions.
- ☐ Modify assignments as directed by the special education teacher or the general education teacher.
- ☐ Make on-the-spot adaptations to curriculum and instruction according to pre-established guidelines.
- ☐ Administer tests individually reinforcing skills that the teacher previously taught.
- ☐ Read aloud to the students.
- ☐ Assist with organizational skills.
- ☐ Create educational memory games and activities.
- ☐ Keep records to document behavior of individual students.
- ☐ Maintain a daily journal or log communicating with parents or other classroom teachers regarding class work, homework, or daily activities.
- ☐ Facilitate social opportunities and interactions for all students.
- ☐ Supervise student who might leave the classroom for a break or might leave to go to another classroom.
- ☐ Check for work completion and homework.
- ☐ Copy notes occasionally or assist with note taking.
- ☐ Support student when involved with group work.
- ☐ Cue/refocus/redirect student.
- ☐ Create review worksheets.
- ☐ Assist with the testing process.
- ☐ Use Boardmaker® by Mayer-Johnson[4] or find clipart pictures to assist student's ability to communicate.
- ☐ Create a "find and point" communication tool for the student.
- ☐ Help create "social stories" for student (autistic spectrum).
- ☐ Create a picture schedule list, color-coded, and teach the student to be as independent as possible with this schedule.

---

[4] http://www.mayer-johnson.com/boardmaker-software

Small Group Assistance

Classroom Teacher:
Subject:

- ☐ Substitute activities without changing curriculum.
- ☐ Adapt instructional materials in accordance with the IEP.
- ☐ Provide remedial instruction and reinforcement skills.
- ☐ Assist the students with individual activities.
- ☐ Help students with makeup work.
- ☐ Assist students with interpreting and following directions.
- ☐ Make on-the-spot adaptations to curriculum and instruction according to pre-established guidelines.
- ☐ Assist with organizational skills.
- ☐ Check for work completion or homework.
- ☐ Create educational memory games and activities.
- ☐ Conduct learning activities as directed by the classroom teacher.
- ☐ Facilitate social opportunities and interactions.
- ☐ Support students involved with group work.
- ☐ Cue, refocus, or redirect students.
- ☐ Read aloud to students.
- ☐ Review for tests.
- ☐ _____.
- ☐ _____.
- ☐ _____.
- ☐ _____.
- ☐ _____.
- ☐ _____.
- ☐ _____.
- ☐ _____.

Social/Behavioral Assistance

Classroom Teacher:
Subject:
Student Initials:

Behavioral Assistance
☐ Cue, refocus, or redirect students.
☐ Implement position control (positioning oneself in the classroom as a behavior management strategy).
☐ Help create "social stories" for students in the autistic spectrum.
☐ Assist with classroom management by implementing class rules.
☐ Keep records to document behavior of individual students.
☐ Supervise students who might leave the classroom for break or might leave to go to another classroom.
☐ Supervise individual students or groups of students at various times of day, such as lunch, recess, or when the teacher is out of the room.
☐ Supervise students during lunch, recess, assemblies, or when getting on or off the bus.
☐ _____.
☐ _____.
☐ _____.

Social Assistance
☐ Create a picture schedule list, color-coded, and teach the student to be as independent as possible with this schedule.
☐ Enlist peers to help a student gather and carry materials.
☐ Facilitate social opportunities and interactions for all students.
☐ _____.
☐ _____.
☐ _____.
☐ _____.

Academic Assistance

Classroom Teacher:
Subject:
Student Initials:

- ☐ Support student in getting ready for in-class assignments or other activities so he or she can keep up with the class while, at the same time, learning how to become more independent.
- ☐ Monitor the student's level of participation in the classroom.
- ☐ Help the classroom teacher with instructional strategies or other supports that are required in the IEP.
- ☐ Adapt instructional materials in accordance with the IEP.
- ☐ Provide remedial instruction and reinforcement skills.
- ☐ Assist students with individual activities.
- ☐ Help students with makeup work.
- ☐ Assist students with interpreting and following directions.
- ☐ Modify assignments for specific students as directed by the special education teacher or the general education teacher.
- ☐ Make on-the-spot adaptations to curriculum and instruction according to pre-established guidelines.
- ☐ Administer tests individually.
- ☐ Reinforce skills that the teacher previously taught.
- ☐ Read aloud to the students.
- ☐ Assist with organizational skills.
- ☐ Check for work completion or homework.
- ☐ Conduct learning activities as directed by the classroom teacher for a small group of students.
- ☐ Maintain a daily journal or log communicating with parents or other classroom teachers regarding class work, homework, or daily activities.
- ☐ Copy notes occasionally or assist with note taking.
- ☐ Support students involved with group work.
- ☐ Make copies of notes.
- ☐ Create review worksheets.
- ☐ Assist with the testing process.
- ☐ Follow-up with the student outside the classroom.
- ☐ Motivate and support students with homework.
- ☐ Work with drop-in center, learning center, or resource room to help students focus and stay on track.
- ☐ Ask questions in class.
- ☐ Answer questions in class.
- ☐ Review for tests with small groups of students.
- ☐ Guide student-centered activities.
- ☐ Serve as a scribe.

Physical Assistance

Classroom Teacher:
Subject:
Student Initials:

☐ Serve as a personal care attendant when appropriate.
☐ Assist with personal hygiene, including feeding and diapering.
☐ Assist students with motor or mobility limitations.
☐ Assist students with individual activities.
☐ Maintain a daily journal or log communicating with parents or other classroom teachers regarding class work, homework, or daily activities.
☐ Supervise students who might leave the classroom for break or might leave to go to another classroom.
☐ Supervise individual students or groups of students at various times of day, such as at lunch, recess, or when the teacher is out of the room.
☐ Supervise students during lunch, recess, assemblies, or when getting on or off the bus. Use Boardmaker® by Mayer-Johnson[5] or find clipart pictures to assist student's ability to communicate.
☐ Create a "find and point" communication tool for the student.
☐ Serve as a scribe.
☐ _____.
☐ _____.
☐ _____.
☐ _____.
☐ _____.
☐ _____.
☐ _____.
☐ _____.
☐ _____.
☐ _____.

---

[5] http://www.mayer-johnson.com/boardmaker-software

Teacher Support

(Not Hired Specifically for Special Education Needs)
Classroom Teacher:
Subject:

- ☐ Help the classroom teacher with instructional strategies or other supports that are required in the IEP.
- ☐ Conduct learning activities as directed by the classroom teacher for a small group of students.
- ☐ Make instructional materials for the whole class so that the teacher can work with individual students.
- ☐ Supervise individual students or groups of students at various times of day, such as at lunch, recess, or when the teacher is out of the room.
- ☐ Supervise students during lunch, recess, assemblies, or when getting on or off the bus.
- ☐ Make copies of notes.
- ☐ Create review worksheets.
- ☐ Assist with the testing process.
- ☐ Answer questions in class.
- ☐ Implement position control (positioning oneself in the classroom as a behavior management strategy).
- ☐ Guide student-centered activities.
- ☐ Assist with classroom management by implementing classroom rules.
- ☐ _____.
- ☐ _____.
- ☐ _____.
- ☐ _____.
- ☐ _____.
- ☐ _____.
- ☐ _____.

Strategies for Collaborative Relationships

In my professional experience, the most effective way to meet the needs of students on an IEP in the general classroom is to seek out ways that the general classroom teacher can implement adaptations quickly and easily. An adaptation that works for all students in the classroom and does not reduce content will more likely be embraced. Consequently, all students benefit.

Communication: What's Working? Card

Good communication with co-workers and students is critical to successful inclusion. Often, our fears, agendas, and even enthusiasm get in the way of doing the kind of listening we need to do to foster good communication. Without effective communication, we make many assumptions about the people with whom we interact. (Friend, 2014b)

Those assumptions might be very inaccurate and create tremendous conflict. Try to keep an open mind. Express how you feel and listen to hear other points of view. Good communication is necessary for the success of an inclusive classroom.

```
It's Working!

Not Working ☹

Let's Try ....
```

This card is a simple way to give feedback to your co-workers or individual members of the teaching team. I found it to be useful for reinforcing the positives. It can be delivered in person, or placed in a teacher mailbox. Simple 3" X 5" index cards work well.

Tips for Successful Collaboration

- Be flexible
- Look for success not only in academic areas
- Make time to plan - even if just 10 minutes!
- Discuss problems only with each other
- Avoid using red ink to write notes to your colleague

Pick-me-ups, Pick-you-ups

- Compliment your colleague where all can see
- Send a letter of appreciation and cc the principal
- Remember special days with cards

When in Conflict

- Change negative self-talk to positive
- Next time X happens...I'll do Y or Z
- Plan viable solutions
- Consider personality type
- Seek suggestions from a supportive colleague or read Albert Ellis for suggestions to reframe
- Visualize yourself in the interaction BEING SUCCESSSFUL!
- Affirm: "I CAN handle this situation"

What Do I Say When My Colleague Says...''?

Trust & Respect:

- What happens in Vegas stays in Vegas.
- Approach from a position of care.
- Be clear about what you want to say.
- Operate from a belief that encourages taking risks.
- Listen to understand, not to judge.
- Validate and appreciate to focus on the positive and make statements in the positive.
- Statements are specific and reflect what is valued by the other person.

Prepare for Communication:

When communicating, always be prepared.

- Have a game plan so that your emotions don't get the best of you.
- Never address a difficulty with your colleague in front of a group, especially your students. It should always be one-to-one.

Active Listening

- Active listening can increase a person's comfort, interest, and motivation(Bodie, Vickery, Cannava, & Jones, 2015).
- Communicate to the speaker that you value him/her as a person.
- Gain an understanding of the speaker's experience (ask questions to learn).
- Communicate that understanding to the speaker so that they feel heard and understood.

Active listening, as the name suggests, is an active process. As you listen to the person speak, and watch their facial expressions and body language, you're actively asking yourself the following three questions:

- What is or was this person feeling?
- What exactly did this person experience?
- What did this person do?

Understanding the Speaker

Periodically, you're asking yourself a fourth question that integrates these:

- What is it like to be in his/her shoes?
- What's the essence, the core message, of what's happening to this person?

What Can We Say? Scripts that Work

Choose Words Strategically

Words to Lose/Use

Lose	Use
■ But	■ And
■ Should	■ Next Time
■ Have To	■ Please
■ Can't	■ Can
■ Don't	■ Do
■ Never	■ specifics

Notice "all," "never," "always," etc., and ask to get more specificity -- often these words are arbitrary limits on behavior. Be specific -- avoid general comments and clarify pronouns such as "it," "that," etc. Be very careful with advice. Susanne Gaddis, PhD, the Communications Doctor, writes:

Adopting, the "words to use...words to lose" (Horn, 2004) *philosophy can work miracles for improving one's interpersonal communication. The basic idea behind this philosophy is that some words and phrases build relationships up, and some words and phrases tear relationships down. Since effective communication is about building and maintaining relationships, we need to choose our words wisely. "Words to use...words to lose" simply facilitates a stronger, more positive emotional vocabulary.*

As we carefully choose words and phrases, it's a good idea to keep in mind that in addition to words having dictionary definitions (their denotations); words also have connotations, which is their emotional impact.

For example, have you ever noticed that successful real estate agents sell homes rather than houses? A house by nature has no personality, is cold, sterile, and devoid of love. Conversely, a home is a warm and loving place, where cookies are baked and where you would find huge piles of laundry waiting to be done. Home gathers its considerable emotional power for the simple reason that it is inhabited in a way that a house is not.

Similarly, the phrases that you mention all bring about a certain feeling or emotional response.

Phrases That Shift the Dynamic Without Escalating Conflict

- What can I do to support you?
- How can I help make this challenge easier for you?
- Can we talk about something I think might help us work together better?
- I'd like to talk about...with you, but first I'd like to get your point of view.
- I think we may have different ideas about... I'd really like to hear your thinking on this and share my perspective as well.

The One- or Two-syllable Response

Statement: I can't possibly see how co-teaching will work.
Sample Responses:

- Really?
- I see
- Oh...

Ask a Question

Statement: This activity is inappropriate for...
Sample Response: What do you mean by "inappropriate"? (Have research available)

Agree in Part and Ask a Question

Statement: This won't work without time to plan.
Sample Response: You're right. We have no common planning time. How can we make the best of our situation?

Agree and Insist (Don't Say, "But...")

Statement: I can't see how we can work together – we are so different!
Sample Response: I would say the same thing if I were you. And we still have the problem of being assigned to this...

Adapted from *Transforming Anger to Personal Power* (S. G. Fitzell, 2007)

Shifting our Mindset: Internal Control

Principles of Human Behavior

- You cannot change others (Ellis, 1999); you can provide the environment, skills, etc.
- People do things for their reasons, not ours.
- We are all different...
- Relationships should complement and complete each other.

Offline Coping Techniques

- Don't take their behavior or words personally.
- Write down details of what annoys you.
- Think about why it annoys you.
- Which of your buttons does this person push?
- Why do you respond to them in the way you do?

Adapted from *Transforming Anger to Personal Power* (S. G. Fitzell, 2007)

The most challenging aspect of working with other adults in the same space is keeping things in perspective. So often, we take things personally that have absolutely nothing to do with us. Another person's behavior can be completely unrelated to anything we've said or done. It's often, simply about "them." Try to keep that frame of reference. It will make life a whole lot easier!

Chapter 2 Review & Discussion Questions

Collaboration Approaches

1. What collaborative relationships do you have in your day-to-day work on campus?
2. What techniques might you use to improve or maintain these relationships?
3. If you are a co-teacher, what collaboration approach(s) work best for you and your teaching partner?
4. Whether you are co-teaching or not, which ideas or strategies support collaboration with colleagues in your professional community?
5. What ideas, insights, or solutions have you formulated, after having read the chapter, that will enhance collaborative relationships within your school community?

Paraprofessionals

If you work with a paraprofessional, what tasks, of those discussed, might that adult do to help facilitate a better learning experience in your classroom?

Practical Application

Demonstrate understanding by creating a script of a dialogue you might have with a colleague or parent that addresses a difficult conversation you've encountered.

✄ **CHAPTER 3** ✑

Classroom Management Techniques

Be a Positive Role Model for Behavior Management[6]

Role-modeling appropriate behavior is a vital and necessary component of an effective approach to behavior management.

Who we are, what we think, and what we believe is revealed through our words and behavior. If we buy into the adage "boys will be boys," our words and behavior will reflect it. If we have prejudices, they will be apparent.

Young people are more likely to do what we do, rather than what we say, and therefore it is vitally important to be self-aware and change our attitudes, beliefs and behaviors to reflect the image we want our youth to model.

For example, sometimes as teachers, parents, or adults in authority, we do not realize how we speak to children. Our tone of voice and choice of words, especially when disciplining, may be reinforcing negative patterns of behavior with children. This became glaringly obvious to me in my early years as a parent as I listened to my seven-year-old when she was angry with me. I often heard my words, my tone, and saw my facial expressions coming from her little body.

Another important part of being a positive role model for young people is showing them respect. Lack of respect from our youth is a common complaint heard from adults today. I am often astounded, however, by the lack of respect some adults show toward young people.

Youth are often treated as lesser beings. Children are ordered around without a "please" or a "thank you." Because they are defenseless, they are often the scapegoats of misplaced anger. Their needs are often disregarded.

All of us may be guilty of disrespecting our children's rights sometimes when we are tired, frustrated, or angry. It must be the exception, not the rule. When we do treat young people in a disrespectful way, the most empowering thing we can do for our children, and for ourselves, is to admit we made a mistake.

When we admit our errors to young people, we teach them that it is okay to make mistakes. Mistakes are for learning. We are modeling a willingness to be honest, to own our behavior, and to learn from it. This is a powerful example to set for our

---

[6] - Excerpted from *Paraprofessionals and Teachers Working Together* (S. Fitzell, 2010)

youth. We want the same behavior from them when they make a mistake. Should we expect less of ourselves?

Each teacher has his or her own preference for class structure, consistency, and management. While it is important to understand that teachers must be free to be themselves and have their own styles of running their classroom, some teaching styles seem to lend themselves well to inclusive populations, where others are more challenging for both students and teachers.

Consider:
- Consistency without rigidity
- Firm discipline without power struggles
- Reasonable flexibility without lax standards
- The goal of the lesson rather than the specifics of the process
- Learning as the goal, rather than focusing on "that" test grade (Re-take a test?)

Physical Structure and Environmental Variables

- Change student seating (closer to center of instruction, closer to teacher, away from friends, away from distracters). Consider allowing a student to choose to change his/her seating as part of a win-win behavior plan. The student owns the behavior and the solution.
- Increase distance between desks and provide more space if possible.
- Scan the room frequently and stay alert to what students are engaged in at all times.
- Consider student's individual needs: vision issues, hearing issues, focus, and comfort levels.
- Avoid seating students with learning disabilities together in the room as permanent seating. It singles them out for stigmatization (the "stupid" group) and creates a situation where they may feed off each other behaviorally.

The Technique that Changed My Teacher Life

Proactive Behavior Plans

*Note: The text below was excerpted from *Free the Children: Conflict Education for Strong Peaceful Minds* (S. G. Fitzell, 1997) and is geared toward ages K-12. The term "child" refers to older students and teens as well as younger children. This approach is very effective with adolescents.

Reality Therapy (Glasser, 1999; Wubbolding, 2007)is a method of counseling developed by William Glasser, MD. This method of therapy is based on Choice Theory (Glasser, 1999), and the goal of counseling is to teach people how to take control of their own lives, make more effective choices, and develop the strength to handle daily stresses and problems. At its foundation is the idea that regardless of what has happened to us or what choices we have made in the past, we can make different choices today and in the future to help us meet our basic needs. By making choices to change behavior, we can change our thinking and feelings.

Choice Theory is based on the fundamental belief that all humans choose behaviors in an attempt to fulfill five basic needs. According to Glasser, these needs are built into our genetic structure. Glasser identifies these basic needs as Love/Belonging, Freedom, Fun, Power, and Survival. Given this theory, human behavior is determined to be internally motivated. Therefore, the only person's behavior we can control is our own.

Although each of us possesses the same five basic human needs, each of us fulfills these needs differently. We develop an inner 'picture album' of how we see the world and what we want that world to be. Our behavior is an attempt to create the ideal world of our 'picture album.' A parent or teacher's goal is to get students to evaluate their present behavior and determine whether it is meeting their needs.

In one example, a teacher or parent might ask a child, "Is your behavior getting you what you want?" If the child is talking constantly in class and, as a consequence, loses his recess, the child who wants Love/Belonging is not getting what he wants through his behavior. On the contrary, he is losing that very thing at recess. If the child is not getting what he needs with his present behavior, he will make a specific plan for change and make a commitment to follow through.

The goal is for the child to determine that his current behavior is not getting him what he wants, and for *him* to choose other behaviors that will better meet his needs. The adult in the situation does *not* do the choosing for the child. The adult may offer suggestions to help the child come up with solutions, but, ultimately, the child must make the choice and commit to it. In this way, the child owns his behavior and the consequences of that behavior. The child cannot come back later and say to the adult, "You did this to me!" or "It's your fault." The child has ownership. Ownership is a critical step in effective discipline and moral growth.

I have found the behavior management approach based on this theory quite successful in the classroom. It utilizes an approach that promotes self-discipline, problem solving, and moral growth. A time-out procedure is used in the behavior management model. This time-out procedure may seem unworkable in school situations where a time-out room or area is not available.

I have found that meeting with students before school and/or after school to work out solutions and develop "Both Win Discipline Plans" can lead to fruitful results. Be creative. Another argument against this method is that it is time-consuming. It is...in the beginning. Be willing to put in the time upfront. It will pay off in the end.

Basic Discipline Format

- *First Offense:* Ask the student, "What are you doing? Is it against the rules? Can you follow the rules?" If the answers are acceptable, student and teacher resume their roles in the class.
- *Second Offense:* Same procedure.
- *Third Offense:* Ask the same questions, except end with the consequence: "You will need to make a [discipline] plan." Assign time to work out a plan with you. (Detention with teacher after school, before school, or during a study/lunch period. Detention lasts as long as it takes to make the plan, whether it's five minutes or repeated detentions over several days – as long as it takes to develop an effective plan.)
- *OPTIONAL:* Sometimes students need to be removed from the room. Arrange with administration to have a time-out area for students to "chill." It is often best to not have administration interfere, but rather to support your efforts to work out the issue with the student yourself through the behavior planning process.

*Do not get pulled into bantering with the student. Do the steps above and walk away. Stick to the script.

Guidelines for Discussion: Win-Win Discipline Plan[7]

Questions to Be Addressed:

What is the Problem? Or *what were you doing that was unacceptable?*
In Reality Therapy, the real question is "What is the Problem?" I found this question led to an answer like, "There's no problem!" For me, "What were you doing that was unacceptable?" is a more direct, less vague, and more productive question. The purpose here is to list the specific behaviors that are causing the problem. Try to avoid confronting values, attitudes, and cultural beliefs.

Whose expectations are not being met?
This question is not on the plan, but it needs to be a part of the discussion. If it is the student's own expectations, you might start with, "I'm concerned..." If it is the parent or teacher's expectations regarding rules, etc., state, "Part of my job as a (parent/teacher) is to mention..." or "to keep you safe..." or "to create a safe environment," etc. If the problem involves others' expectations, you might say, "I'm hearing things that concern me, and I want..."

What do you want as a result of the conversation?
State what you want as a result of the discussion. Word what you want in the form of a solution. "I want to work out a way that 'X' happens..." or "I want to figure out a way that we both win: that you get _____, and I get _____." Do not get sucked into arguing about the problem. Kids are experts at avoiding responsibility and resolution by bantering, badgering, blaming, and "Yeah, but...!"

What will the resolution include?
The resolution might include 1) a plan for the future, 2) no plan (just a sharing of feelings, or 3) if there is a plan, a) logical consequences, or, b) no consequences. The plan must include a commitment. If it doesn't, then a new plan must be worked out that the child can commit to.

Note: When children are resistant to planning, I simply tell them that they will continue with time-out (whether that means consecutive detentions, discussions, time-outs, internal suspensions, etc.) until we 'work it out' and create a plan that we both feel comfortable with. If the plan involves restitution, it must also be acceptable to the 'victim.'

---

[7] The Win-Win Discipline Plan and Guidelines are based on my experience using principles of Reality Therapy and Choice Theory. They have not been endorsed by the Institute for Reality Therapy.

Win-Win Discipline Plan

NAME: DATE:

What were you doing that was unacceptable?

Was your behavior against the rules of the class or the school? _____ Explain:

Was your behavior helping you? _____ Explain:

Was your behavior helping your teacher? _____ Explain:

Are you willing to try a different behavior? _____
What could you have done differently in **this** situation:

What is your plan to follow the rules of the class (or school)? What will you change or improve? List things you **will do** rather than things you will not do. Be specific.

Are you willing to *accept* your plan and *stick with it*? _____

List the consequences for not following through on your plan.

Signatures:

Student: Teacher:

PLAN REVIEW DATE: Follow-up notes:

Strategies for Effective Group Processes

Establish Ground Rules.

In order for students to behave appropriately and stay on task during small group work, they have to be taught how to work in a group. Students have been trained over the years to sit at desks lined up in rows and passively receive information. Many, if not most, students have no idea how to work in a group. If they have experience with group work it might be quite limited because schools still teach primarily through a direct teaching, whole class model. So, when students are suddenly asked to work in a group they often misbehave and mismanage their time. They simply don't know how to do small group work.

Consequently, teachers need to teach students how to work in a group. The first step in the process is to establish ground rules and norms for interaction. These are the guidelines that must be enforced by teachers and students themselves in order for group work to be effective. Ground rules should encourage positive collaborative behaviors among all students. In my experience, students abide by rules best when they have a part in making them. Janice Whatley, Salford Business School, using an interpretive case study approach to analyzing student teams, discovered a positive benefit of encouraging teams to agree on ground rules at the start of their projects (Whatley, 2009).

Ground rules need to be posted in the classroom so students can readily refer to them. If students or teachers believe that additional rules are needed, they can be added later.

A very effective technique for teaching students appropriate small group behavior is to have students take an active role in identifying what appropriate behavior actually looks like. It's worth taking the time to do some role-play with the students to show the difference between an ineffective group and an effective group. Another very effective strategy is to have students give their input on inappropriate behavior, for example, putting other students down in the group or laughing at group members ideas. Students are more likely to comply if they have agreed with reasonable behavior and consequences.

Some Suggested Ground Rules:

- Start on time.
- Practice respect for yourself and others.
- Come prepared to do your part.
- Be a good listener.
- No put-downs.
- Make sure everyone gets a chance to contribute or speak.
- Accept constructive criticism gracefully.
- Critique ideas, not people.
- Stay on task.
- No interruptions; let people finish talking.
- Ask for help when you're confused about what to do.
- Help others when you can.
- Do your fair share of the work.

Establish Teacher Expectations for Small Group Work

- Describe, show an example, or model the expectations for assignments and activities.
- Provide models and examples of what the outcome should, and should not, look like.
- Rehearse the expectations.
- Notice positive group behavior.
- Correct misbehavior and teach appropriate behavior and expectations. (We cannot assume that students know what to do.)
- Review expectations frequently.

Introducing the Group Activity

- Arrange tasks so that all students are within the teacher's view.
- Be thorough when explaining instructions and giving directions.

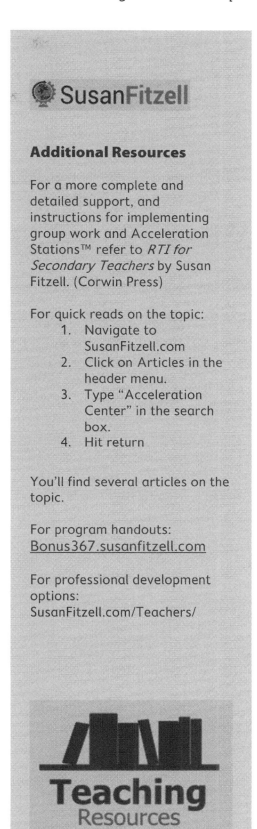

Additional Resources

For a more complete and detailed support, and instructions for implementing group work and Acceleration Stations™ refer to *RTI for Secondary Teachers* by Susan Fitzell. (Corwin Press)

For quick reads on the topic:
1. Navigate to SusanFitzell.com
2. Click on Articles in the header menu.
3. Type "Acceleration Center" in the search box.
4. Hit return

You'll find several articles on the topic.

For program handouts:
Bonus367.susanfitzell.com

For professional development options:
SusanFitzell.com/Teachers/

- Make sure students understand what they are going to do and why they are going to do it.
- Be clear in stating teacher expectations.
- Establish time limits and provide checkpoints within those time limits. For example, if students are going to work in small groups for 15 minutes, check in with students as a whole class to make sure they are on track every three to four minutes.
- Describe and model the final product.
- Monitor small groups and provide guidance as needed.

Develop a Class Plan for Differentiating Within Groups

Consider:
- How will the class be rearranged when necessary? What will be required to accomplish rearranging the classroom?
- What routines and skills are necessary for students to learn to have the class run smoothly when we deviate from the traditional row arrangement? Have students practice moving from one room arrangement to another.
- Use a signal, either a hand gesture or a sound, to notify students of time remaining until a transition, then use the signal again when the transition needs to occur. Before any transition, remind students of behavioral expectations.
- Ensure that each student has a job to do and a rubric to measure their own performance.
- Each member of the group must be accountable as individual participants and as collaborators in the group.
- Each member of the group needs clear expectations as to what to do when they perceive their "job" as done. They must understand that their job is not done until the entire group has completed the assigned tasks or project.

Much research has been done on the success and failure of group work. In order for group work and cooperative learning to succeed, it's important to set clear expectations for success. It's also critical that the expectations and logistics be explicitly taught. We cannot assume that students know how to behave in groups.(McGlynn & Kozlowski, 2016)

Strategies that Promote Positive Behavior

Use Music to Enhance the Learning Environment

Mozart for Modulation

Music to Enhance Attention and Learning, Selections by Sheila Frick, OTR – Audio CD https://goo.gl/1DYiyg
- Helps with attention issues and sensory processing difficulties
- Supports organized body movement
- Improves attention and spatial concepts
- Assists active engagement of the learner

It's the complexity of the music that makes Mozart effective. (Demorest & Morrison, 2000; Jausovec et al., 2006)

How to Choose and Use Music in Your Classroom

Playing music can be a distraction, especially when students are reading. Here are some guidelines:

1. Select a CD to fit the project your students are engaged in doing:

    - Learning, Concentration, and Thinking – 50-60 beats per minute (b.p.m.) for study, testing, workgroups, and computer time.
    - De-Stress and Relax – 30-60 b.p.m. for settling the class after high energy activities or disruptions, or rest times.
    - Inspiration – 60-90 b.p.m. for creative work.
    - Motivation – 120-140 b.p.m.; Productivity – 70-130 b.p.m. for task completion and kinesthetic activities.

2. Keep the volume low. You should not have to 'talk above' the music. The music should be in the background, creating a filter for unwanted noise in the classroom throughout the day. This creates the "body relaxed, mind alert" state.

3. For a break after 45 minutes or more of studying, you may increase the volume a bit so students may listen to the music for a few minutes. This technique is recommended in the book "Learn with the Classics" by Anderson, Marsh and Harvey. It is meant to relax students and let their minds reflect on what they have learned.

Adapted from Advanced Brain Technologies, LLC (ABT), http://www.advancedbrain.com/ – products available at this site.

Suggested Music Selections:

- Harp (i.e. Hilary Stagg)
- Native American Flute (i.e. Andrew Vasquez, R. Carlos Nakai)
- Mellow Jazz (i.e. Kenny G)
- Enya
- Yanni
- Michael Jones' Magical Child

Enhance the Lighting in your Classroom

You may have never thought about the lighting in your classroom, but lighting can be used to enhance the learning experience and can have a significant impact on the learning environment. (Cooper, 1999; Sleep, 2008; Vandewalle et al., 2010) Surprisingly, lighting can even affect test scores; studies have shown that students who are exposed to more natural light in the classroom – a practice known as "daylighting" – score higher on standardized tests than those in more traditional classroom environments.

The fluorescent lighting used in most classrooms can lead to a host of difficulties, including migraines (Robert, 2008) and harsh grey-toned light, not to mention the distractions of flickering or buzzing lights. By introducing more natural lighting into the classroom, we're working with the body's natural circadian rhythms to indicate to the brain that it's time to be awake and alert. Studies have also theorized that natural lighting improves visibility, health, mood, and behavior. And students aren't the only ones who benefit – adults in the classroom enjoy the benefits of natural lighting as well!

Unfortunately, a lot of school buildings were built before the 1980s, when research into the positive benefits of light really started. Even if you can't increase the natural light in your classroom, you can approximate natural daylight by using full-spectrum lighting as well as increasing blue lighting (natural daylight includes a lot of blue light).

Depending on your school's rules and your community's rules from the fire department, here are a few ways to improve the lighting in your classroom:

- Replace fluorescent lighting bulbs with full-spectrum bulbs.
- Use lamps in the classroom with full-spectrum light bulbs.
- Cover fluorescents with curtains made from pajamas made from fire-retardant material.
- If your classroom has drop ceilings, cover the clear panels under the fluorescents with heat-resistant blue spray paint (of course, you will need to discuss this with your school's administration before painting school property!)
- Put blue fluorescent light protectors over fluorescent bulbs.

Blue light protectors can be purchased online; refer to the World Wide Web Resources in the back of this book for retailers.

One teacher in my seminar uses heat-resistant stained glass paint to cover fluorescents in the classroom. Although not scientifically proven, this method does help reduce harsh glare from normal fluorescent bulbs. Other teachers have used heat-resistant blue spray paint to cover the lights.

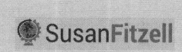

Additional Resources

This chapter provides many strategies that motivate students to choose success.

For a more complete and detailed support, get Susan's Solution Series book, *Motivating Students to Choose Success: Proven Strategies to Lend a Helping Hand*

Go to Shop.SusanFitzell.com

Also, navigate to SusanFitzell.com for helpful articles on behavior management, conflict resolution, bullying prevention, and motivation.

For program handouts: Bonus367.susanfitzell.com

For professional development options: SusanFitzell.com/Teachers/

Standing Stations in Your Classroom!

Do you have students who can't sit still in class? Do you have a child that can't sit to do homework? I had students who struggled to sit in the classroom and I realized one day that if I allowed them to stand and work off a bookcase or some other appropriately raised platform, they were more focused and behavior significantly improved. When my son was little, he'd eat better if he could stand at the dining room table. It also minimized trips to the hospital because he no longer fell out of his chair.

And as for myself, I can't sit to focus. I actually create a standing station in my office and in my hotel rooms with a lap desk on top of the desk by placing an upside-down drawer or a box on the desk. I am significantly more productive and focused when standing to read, write, or create.

An additional benefit of offering standing stations is the health benefits: studies show a reduction in Body Mass Index (BMI) of students in stand biased classrooms.(Chubbs, 2017)

Using a Points Chart

A point chart is a type of a rubric for behavior expectations. Students understand the requirements for earning points in the rubric. Each day, a tally is taken based on the student's level of performance per the listed expectations. This daily level of accountability helps many students stay on target. For some students, it can provide extra motivation to demonstrate behaviors that support their success.

Class Points Chart

POINTS CHART   Class_____ Period_____

1 POINT FOR EACH: W = writing utensil   P = present on time
N = notebook/textbook   C = class work   B = behavior

STUDENT	MON	TUES	WED	THU	FRI	TOT
1.						
2.						
3.						
4.						
5.						
6.						
7.						
8.						
9.						
10.						
11.						
12.						
13.						
14.						
15.						
16.						
17.						
18.						
19.						
20.						
21.						
22.						
23.						
24.						
25.						
26.						
27.						
28.						

Behavior Management Cue Card

Cue cards are an excellent Instructional tool for teachers in the diverse classroom. Research has indicated that using cue cards with students can support their success both academically and behaviorally. Both students with and without academic challenges benefit from the use of cue cards in educational settings.

This cue card enables teachers to provide students with positive feedback or provide a needed redirection without stigmatizing or embarrassing the student. While using cue cards to redirect students to more positive behavior choices or to prompt recall of instruction, as a positive feedback tool, cue cards empower students by recognizing their effort and success. (Conderman & Hedin, 2015)

Cue cards require modeling and practice prior to implementation to be effective. So, be sure to teach students how they will be used and what is expected in response. Whereas this cue card is ready-made and generic, they can be individualized to student needs.

Cue Card Instructions
1. Create your cue card to match redirection and praise you frequently state in class.
2. Stick the cue card on the top corner of each student's desk. (Laminate it, use shipping tape, etc. to make it sturdy.)
3. Rather than disturb the class with a verbal correction or embarrass a student with verbal praise, walk up to the student's desk and:
   a. Make eye contact.
   b. Point to the picture on the card that represents what you want to say.
   c. Walk away. (Do not say anything or engage in banter.)

Optional: You might also punch a hole in the laminated card and put it on a lanyard or keep it in your pocket. This is especially helpful if you cannot tape the cards to the students' desks.

Cue Card Example

Work Quietly 	Get to work! 	Take out your pencil. 
Open your book. 	High five! 	You should be reading. 
Show Respect. 	You're doing Great! 	Thank you for doing the right thing.  THANK YOU!

Goal Setting: A Proven Motivational Strategy

Goal setting is a planning process that empowers students to take control of their progress and work toward something in which they have invested. Research has indicated goal setting is a predictor of student success. Students who set goals for their academic success achieve more.(Zimmerman, Bandura, & Martinez-Pons, 1992) Students need to choose their own goals. We might guide them in the process; however, if they are to be motivated to work toward the goals, they have to feel ownership.

Long-term goals are good for the big picture; however, they seldom seem to keep students motivated on a day-to-day basis. Short-term goals that work toward the long-term goal seem to keep students on task and allow them to see the milestones accomplished.

Encourage students to commit to realistic and reachable short-term goals. If students are unrealistic, they will fail to reach their goal and thus defeat the process of goal setting. It is important for students to meet their goals to feel successful and not repeat a cycle of failure.

Process Flow Chart for Setting Goals

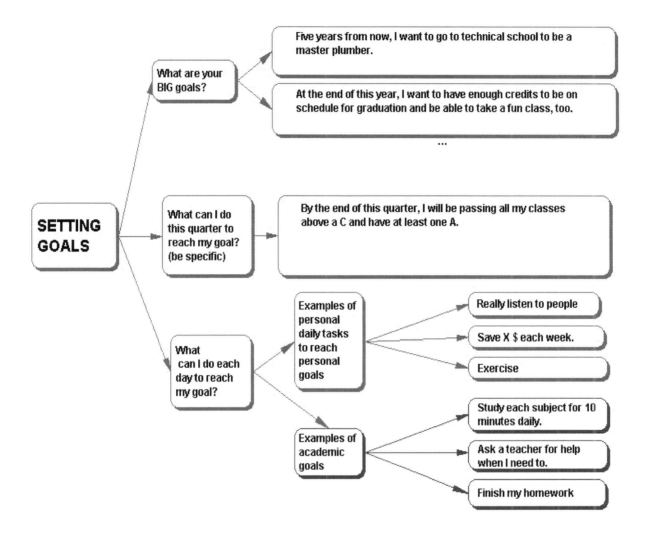

 # REACH FOR THE STARS
(An experience in setting goals)

Today's date_____

THREE THINGS I WILL DO THIS QUARTER (GOALS):

1. _____

2. _____

3. _____

Place a star by the most important one

OBSTACLES TO OVERCOME:

1. _____

2. _____

3. _____

HOW I WILL OVERCOME THE OBSTACLES:

_____

_____

_____

WAS I ABLE TO MEET MY GOAL(S)? _____

IF NOT, WHY NOT?

_____

_____

Chapter 3 Review & Discussion Questions

This chapter discusses three issues:
- Proactive behavior plans
- Strategies for successful group process
- Strategies to promote positive behavior

1. Which of these issues can you, or will you, adjust or address to improve behavior and promote learning in your classroom?
2. Which, if any, of these issues are you unable to address or affect? Why?
3. Given the discussion, tools, and techniques presented, how is your current classroom management approach similar to or different from the ideas presented in the chapter?
4. How will you ensure student buy-in that promotes a win-win environment?
5. What input might students have in the classroom environment? What choices will they be empowered to make?
6. Create a plan to establish clear expectations and logical consequences for behavior that includes and respects student input.
7. How might you utilize the tools and ideas outlined in this section to improve motivation and enhance learning in your classroom?
8. What opportunities for participation in inquiry, self-monitoring, and self-evaluation are regularly promoted in your classroom, currently?
9. How might you take the goal setting activities in the book up a level to include consistent, ongoing student participation in classroom decision making and goal setting?
10. How might strategies such as music, warm lighting techniques, and standing stations promote more positive and focused behavior in the classroom?

Practical Application

Modify your classroom environment based on the conclusions realized during your consideration of the review and discussion questions for this chapter. Observe and record the results of your modifications.

✄ **CHAPTER 4** ✄

Creating Caring Inclusive Communities

The Five Components to Building a Caring Community

Conflict Resolution and Bully Prevention[8]

In my book, *Free The Children: Conflict Education for Strong, Peaceful Minds*, (S. G. Fitzell, 1997) when I refer to conflict, I am referring to interpersonal conflict between two or more people. When I wrote the book, I described what I teach as "conflict education" rather than "conflict resolution." I did so because I believe it is necessary to educate before there is a conflict.

Much of the material available for teaching conflict resolution skills is simply what claims to be: activities that teach skills to deal with issues AFTER there is a conflict. Also, much of the material available is geared toward wide age ranges, encouraging a "pick and choose" approach that does not lend itself to a comprehensive, developmentally-appropriate process.

I refer to a process rather than a program because teaching character and conflict resolution is not something that can be done in a set of isolated lessons in a curriculum program.

Through my research and experience, I have determined that five areas need to be addressed on a *continuous* basis to achieve long-term results from a character and conflict resolution process. These five components are:
- Modeling: Role-modeling for youth
- Relationship: The connections with or between people; how we relate
- Conditioning: The effects of the environment on our youth
- Empowerment
- Skills: Relationship, conflict resolution, and mediation

These five components are critical to an effective character and conflict resolution curriculum. They apply to all developmental levels. Without all five aspects in the curriculum on a consistent basis, long-term results cannot be achieved. These five components are discussed in *Free The Children: Conflict Education for Strong, Peaceful Minds*.

---

[8] Excerpted from *Free The Children: Conflict Education for Strong, Peaceful Minds* by Susan Fitzell, New Society Publishers, 1997.

Establish a 'No Put-Downs' Rule –

A 'Safe Place' Environment

Class rule: No put-downs, no exceptions – not by students or by the teacher.

Considerations & Logic Behind the Rule:

Sarcasm and put-downs have become an acceptable form of entertainment and humor in our society. Because of this cultural acceptance, people, young and old, rationalize that it is okay to denigrate another person in the name of teasing, good fun, and humor. Unfortunately, this belief system causes problems:

- There are people, students included, who cannot read the difference between sarcastic humor and intentional meanness. Many students with learning disabilities are in this group.
- Students learn best in a safe, non-threatening environment. How does the teacher draw the line between what is humor and what is bullying or mean?
- I used to tell my students, "Even if someone laughs at your teasing, how do you really know what they are feeling? Would most students, especially male students, 'show' their hurt?" I talked to a young woman with an eating disorder who shared with me "one line" – what someone said to her in the seventh grade sent her into the spiral of an eating disorder. She could pinpoint the put-down to that moment in time. Also, remember the student shooter in San Diego? He laughed off the put-downs he had to endure. Then he showed up at school with a gun.
- I ask, "How do we know that our words meant in fun are taken as they are meant?" Is it worth the risk?

SusanFitzell

Additional Resources

This chapter provides a general overview of classroom management and authoritative discipline.

For more detailed information about creating caring communities at home and at school, see my book, *Free the Children: Conflict Education for Strong Peaceful Minds*

Shop.SusanFitzell.com

Also, navigate to SusanFitzell.com for helpful articles on behavior management, conflict resolution, bullying prevention, and motivation.

For bullying prevention, navigate to howtopreventbullying.com

and

Facebook.com/ HowToPreventBullying/

Teaching Resources

- What if we encouraged our students to share when words came across as put-downs, even when the person using the put-down is the teacher? What kind of environment would that create in our classrooms?
- Many adults who use sarcastic humor become very defensive when this rule is suggested. Why do you think that is? We need to ask ourselves, "What kind of room do I want to run? What kind of community do I want to create in my classroom? How do I achieve that?"
- People who use sarcasm as humor are not bad people. Rather, they are conditioned by their upbringing or our media culture to enjoy it, accept it, and use it. Awareness is the first step to change.

Bullying in the Classroom: Nip it in the Bud

If bullying is a problem in your classroom, you're not alone. Bullying is a problem in most of the schools I've visited and it's a problem nationwide. However, here's a great way for you to combat bullying in your classroom and actually offer your kids a great lesson at the same time.

The idea is based on something that the New York City Police Department tried in order to combat violent crime, and it actually works wonders in the classroom. Back when Rudy Giuliani was the mayor of New York, he made it his business to turn the tide against violent crime. However, instead of going after the major offenders, he went after the petty thieves, the vandals, the pickpockets, and those who affected quality of life. He theorized that by cutting down on petty crime, he could cut down on violent crime as well. The idea worked brilliantly and New York is now one of the safest large cities in the country(Barrett, 2001).

I spoke with a teacher who tried a similar approach in her classroom. Instead of focusing on the blatant bullying that occurred in the school, she focused on the little things. For example, she addressed name calling every time she caught it. When kids referred to someone as being a "loser," even though most would consider that a minor offense, she used it as a teachable moment and explained how that language hurts. She realized that if she could get her kids to use positive language rather than negative language, the idea of bullying would be less appealing to them as well, and would be less tolerated.

She got results! By modeling to her kids how to act positively and demanding that they do the same, she has virtually eliminated bullying in her 6th grade classroom! If you try this idea and it works for you as well, please let me know, as I'd love to hear about your success.

Emotions and Learning

It is important for students to have time to deal with their emotions. Teenagers are often ruled by their emotions. Emotions override their good judgment, dominate their peer relationships, and physically exhaust them. If they find a new love, their world is an emotional high. If they break up with a boyfriend or girlfriend, their distress can be all-consuming. Arguments can become volatile. Protests are passionate. The fight for independence is powered by intense emotion. When teens are in a state of extreme emotion, it is difficult for them to focus on academics or household responsibilities. Often, they simply cannot function beyond talking endlessly with friends about their feelings or withdrawing to their room to sleep or listen to music.

A little patience and care can go a long way when teens are overpowered by the turmoil of their emotions. In the classroom, try to foster an environment where teens feel comfortable enough to ask for what they need, whether that means seeing a guidance counselor, the nurse, or a trip to the lavatory to pull themselves together.

It's easy for us to trivialize some of the problems about which teenagers get upset. To teenagers, however, their problems are all-consuming. Their emotions are intense. They don't have the maturity to keep these things in perspective. They need us to be understanding, to give them space to deal with these emotions, but also to set boundaries and limits so we are not victims of their outbursts and they are protected from clouded judgment.

Strategies that Foster Caring Communities

Cooperative Learning

What is It?

Cooperative learning is a successful teaching strategy in which small teams, each with students of different levels of ability, use a variety of learning activities to improve their understanding of a subject. Each member of a team is responsible not only for learning what is taught but also for helping teammates learn, thus creating an atmosphere of achievement.

Why Use It?

Documented results include improved academic achievement, improved behavior and attendance, increased self-confidence and motivation, and increased liking of school and classmates. Cooperative learning is also relatively easy to implement and is inexpensive.

How Does It Work?

Here are some typical strategies that can be used with any subject, in almost any grade, and without a special curriculum:

 GROUP INVESTIGATIONS are structured to emphasize higher-order thinking skills such as analysis and evaluation. Students work to produce a group project, which they may have a hand in selecting.

STAD (Student Teams-Achievement Divisions) is used in grades 2-12. Students with varying academic abilities are assigned to 4- or 5-member teams in order to study what the teacher has initially taught and to help each reach his or her highest level of achievement. Students are then tested individually. Teams earn certificates or other recognition based on the degree to which all team members have progressed over their past records.

JIGSAW II is used with narrative material in grades 3-12. Each team member is responsible for learning a specific part of a topic. After meeting with members of other groups, who are "expert" in the same part, the "experts" return to their own groups and present their findings. Team members then are quizzed on all topics (Balkom, 1992)

The benefits of cooperative learning, as shown in research, include (Marzano Debra J. Pollock, Jane E., Marzano, Pickering, & Pollock, 2001):

- Improvements in academic achievement
- Increased self-confidence & motivation
- Improved critical thinking skills
- Increased enthusiasm about school
- Greater teamwork among students
- Lower absenteeism

A resource for cooperative learning and inclusion:
Cooperative Learning and Strategies for Inclusion: Celebrating Diversity in the Classroom. 2nd ed. Edited by JoAnne W. Putnam, Ph.D. Baltimore, MD: Brookes Publishing Co., 1998.
ISBN 1-55766-346-7.

This 288-page book is intended to help educators meet the needs of children with varying cognitive abilities, developmental and learning disabilities, sensory impairments, and different cultural, linguistic, and socioeconomic backgrounds. It is based on the premise that children of differing abilities and backgrounds will benefit both academically and socially from cooperative learning. Available at http://www.brookespublishing.com.

Peer Tutoring

One of the most successful approaches I have used in the Inclusion classroom to reinforce material is peer tutoring. Ten to fifteen minutes a few times a week can make a significant difference in student test results. Students work with each other on a one-to-one basis to reinforce vocabulary, content area facts, or application of material. There exists a substantial body of research to support peer tutoring and peer assisted learning (Mcduffie, Mastropieri, & Scruggs, 2009; O'Donnell King, Alison et al., 1999; Palincsar & Herrenkohl, 2002).

Some students initially need instruction on how to peer tutor; however, many students naturally know how to teach their peers. Students generally relate well to their peers, and the social aspects of peer tutoring interaction allow them to feel less drudgery with the study process. In addition, students benefit from the cheerleading, pushing, feedback, and clarification provided by their peers.

Michael Webb in "Peer Helping Relationships in Urban Schools" (Webb, 1987) writes, "As a result of their efforts to help others, tutors reinforce their own knowledge and skills, which in turn builds their self-confidence and self-esteem. Peer tutors also develop a sense of responsibility as a result of helping students to learn. Finally, explaining the subject matter to others often helps tutors better understand it themselves.

Both tutors and students being tutored have also reported improved attitudes toward school as a result of their participation.

"The use of peer tutors in the classroom can make teachers more flexible and enable them to better target their efforts toward individual students. They can introduce learning activities that could not be accommodated within their regular teaching load. Peer tutors, by assuming responsibility for the reinforcement of what has been covered in class by the teacher, or for remedial instruction, can free teachers for new roles as coordinators and facilitators instead of their functioning solely as dispensers of knowledge.

Numerous studies have demonstrated the effectiveness of the peer tutoring relationship. Students in effective programs consistently reach higher levels of academic achievement than students in conventional learning, or mastery learning situations."(Webb, 1987)

In addition to gaining mastery over academic material, peer tutoring offers students the opportunity to participate among their peers in a meaningful role. I have seen students who typically exhibit challenging behavior model caring, focus, attention to detail, and determination to succeed when in a peer tutoring situation. Peer tutoring – youth helping youth – builds self-esteem. It's also an exercise in contributing to society in a positive way, which is a wonderful life lesson.

Strategies for Building Caring Communities

Problem Solving Mind Map

Decision Making Strategy: Problem Solving Flowchart

Who: Student with a problem.
What: The use of the flowchart as a way to brainstorm, analyze, and choose solutions to problems.
When:

- Teacher and student are experiencing a conflict or discipline issue.
- Student must make a decision and is having difficulty doing so. For example, a student must choose courses to take next semester, or must decide what afterschool activity to do; how to handle a difficult situation; or how to choose between any two options.

Why: All too often, students make decisions without thinking through the positive and negative consequences of those decisions. This flowchart allows students to work with an adult to come up with the best solution for the student.

Critical factor: Adults are encouraged to guide the student through this process without passing judgment, or trying to convince the youth that certain pros and cons are better than others, or certain decisions need to be made. It is imperative that the adult help the students come up with pros and cons, but not make the decision for the child or pressure the child to think of things in any one way.

Accommodation: Students may fill this chart out on their own, or an adult may scribe for the student.

I started using this format with students to help them see that there were positive and negative consequences to any solution they presented to a problem they were experiencing. Originally, it was used to help students who were dealing with anger toward another adult or student, and who were gravitating toward poor choices.

For example, a student would come to me upset because another student bullied him. The first solution students would often choose was fighting. So, I would sit down with the student, list the problem on a piece of paper, create a T-chart, and start asking questions. If the first possible solution for that student was to beat up the antagonizer, I would simply write that down at the top of the first T-chart.

Next, I would ask the student to list the advantages of beating up the student they were angry with. Usually they came up with this list quite easily. I happily wrote these solutions down without passing judgment or discouraging their choices. I have learned through years of working with angry adolescents that the last thing they were willing to hear was my lecture on how they should behave and what better choices they might have available.

The next step was to write down the disadvantages of that solution. This is the part where students usually ran into trouble. Oftentimes, they could not think of any disadvantages, or they did not want to admit or list them.

If students could not come up with potential consequences to their solution, I would ask if they would like me to offer possible consequences. Typically, a student would allow me to suggest negative consequences for discussion. Again, I was careful not to get into parental lecture mode. Instead, I would simply list real consequences. And unless the student could provide evidence that that consequence was not a likely threat, they were written down.

Then, without further ado, we went on to another solution and repeated the process. I typically found that having three viable solutions was all that was needed to start discussing which of the solutions provided the student with the best possible outcome.

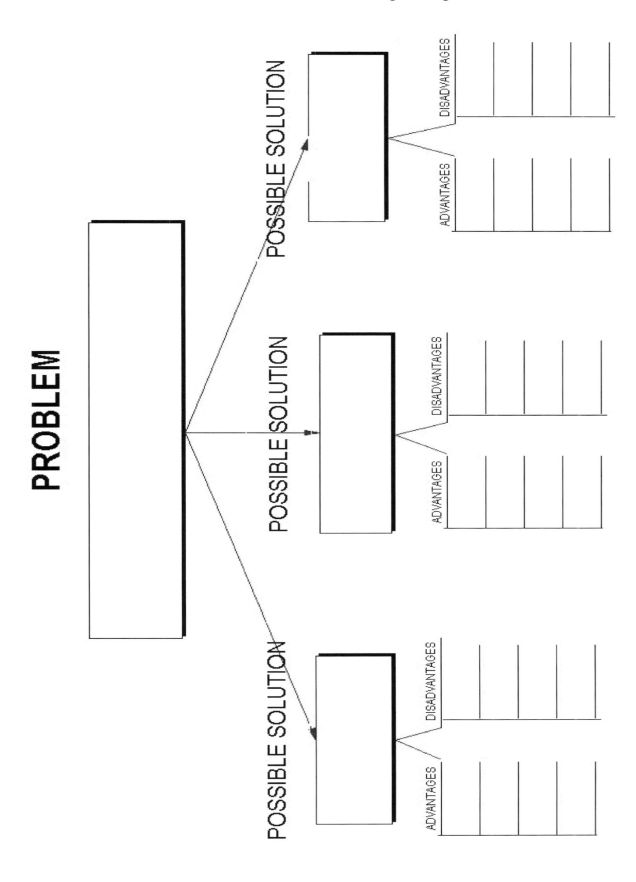

A Dozen Tried & True Ways to Stop Conflict in Its Tracks!

When you find yourself caught in a verbal exchange that does not 'feel' right, then you may be dealing with bullying-- intimidation, bulldozing, sarcasm, pushiness, exploitation, manipulation, etc. You may, also, simply be dealing with someone who is upset over a misunderstanding and unable to communicate clearly in the moment.

What can you do to deal with the situation in the most positive and constructive way? How do you stand up for yourself without being overly aggressive or resorting to language that escalates the conflict? How do you avoid feeling like a victim? Below are a dozen tried & true ways to stop conflict in its tracks and keep your power!

1 Stop, Breathe, Think, and Act
   a Stop & pay attention to your body signals - don't ignore the discomfort, adrenaline rush, etc.
   b Breathe deeply from your belly. Cross your arms and legs and touch your tongue to your pallet as you breathe to engage your brain and limbic system.
   c Think: "I CAN handle this!" (Positive self-talk).
   d Consciously act! (As opposed to Re-Act).

2 Use comebacks that don't escalate Conflict
   a Thank you for letting me know how you feel.
   b I hear you.
   c I can see this upsets you.
   d I'm sorry you were hurt. That was not my intent.
   e Agree with some of the statement but not all. (e.g. "You have a chip on your shoulder because you are short." Agree, "Yes, I am short.")
   f You have an interesting perspective. I'll have to give that some thought.

3 Separate yourself from the situation.
   a I will talk to you when you are calm. (Call "Time", & leave)
   b I will talk to you when I am calm. (Call "Time", & leave)

4 Ask a question; s/he who asks the question has the power.
   a Why does that bother you? How so? Why do you ask? What makes you say that?
   b I know you wouldn't have said that unless you had a good reason.
   c Could you tell me what it was?

d   Be conscious of your body language and the words you choose: Keep Your Power.

5   Be careful about tone of voice. Lower your voice. A soft, confident voice can be very powerful.

6   Avoid "should", "ought", and "you" statements.

7   Use 'I" statements:
   a   When you
   b   I feel
   c   Next time would you

8   Let the other person save face so that they can change their minds. Give them a gracious way out.

9   Stick to the issues. When our 'buttons get pushed' we often lose sight of our goal. Keep the goal in mind.

10 Empathize. Yes, empathize. This is difficult to do and can be very effective at the same time.

11 Make a plan to handle the situation positively in the future.
   a   What will you say? How will you say it? Assess whether it will reduce or escalate conflict.
   b   When you have an assertive response that does not escalate conflict, practice it with a trusted partner.
   c   Visualize & practice the dialogue in your mind's eye. Visualize success.
   d   When that person pushes your buttons the next time, you'll be prepared!

Chapter 4 Review & Discussion Questions

1. After reviewing the information on conflict resolution and bully prevention in this chapter, how might you utilize the tools and ideas outlined to promote a caring, inclusive environment your classroom?
2. What is your plan for modeling and reinforcing social skills and a positive culture in your classroom?
3. How will you provide timely and meaningful feedback of inappropriate behavior?
4. Choose one or two ways to stop conflict in its tracks. Role-play with another adult, or your students to practice using the strategy. Continue revisiting this activity until the response becomes automatic.

Practical Application

Identify and record one concrete example of how you applied the principles, ideas, and strategies outlined in this chapter to foster a more caring community in your classroom or on your campus.

✄ **CHAPTER 5** ☃

Tools and Forms that Support Success

Useful Tools for Planning and Making Adaptations

The forms, examples, ideas and information in this chapter are the result of my experience and the experience of other teachers, working in differentiated classrooms. Every idea, technique, and tool is "classroom proven." As you consider this material, I encourage you to look deeper at each idea for ways that you might adapt these strategies for your own classroom, subject area, or situation.

Classroom & Student Organizers

Supplemental Reinforcement Materials

Create a bulletin board "pocket" resource for students. Include items like the following in the pockets for students to access as needed. This is not only a helpful resource for students, it saves the teacher time because these tools are in one place. Teachers won't spend valuable time looking for these items when they could be doing something else.

Include in the pockets:
- Photocopy of the day's notes
- Mnemonic devices to enhance recall of important information
- Supplemental resources: Related photos, manipulatives, graphs and charts, etc.
- Additional copies of assignments
- Assignment due date calendar
- Whatever else works to scaffold and support student success.

Additional Copy of Assignments

Place extra copies of assignments in a bulletin board pocket or a crate.

 Add to the folders and crates books on topic at lower reading levels, graphic organizers, visuals, study guides, audio tapes, video if available, or any other supplement that can help meet the learning styles and multiple intelligences of your students.

Homework Tip

Designate a consistent "spot" in the classroom for turning in homework and assignments. This simple accommodation can make a world of difference for students in the autistic spectrum and students who "forget" to turn in completed assignments.

Photocopies of Today's Notes

Place a copy of the daily notes in a folder on the bulletin board or in a crate with file folders for each unit. It is a tremendous help to students who were absent, who are slow taking notes, who cannot listen to lecture and copy at the same time, or who are having an exceptionally bad day and consequently miss the notes. I have students "copy" the photocopy unless their IEP says they should not be expected to copy notes.

Assignment Board/Chart

- Printed
- Listed with due dates
- Checkpoints
- Calendar format

OR

- List format

A large write-on/wipe-off wall calendar works very well. A wipe-off calendar purchased at an office supply company will work well for an assignment board or chart. Students can "see" time on a calendar and are less likely to misjudge how much time is left before an assignment is due. Color-code the calendar to match "assignment filled" manila folders in an organizational crate.

Online Homework Bulletin Board

For students and teachers that have access to the Internet at school or home, online homework sites and teacher-made websites provide a wonderful resource for homework.

Not only do students who 'forget' their homework find value in these sites, but so do students who have missed school because of illness, etc.

Parents, also, can use these sites to help support their children with homework completion.

Documents to Keep Up With the IEP

Sample Letter to Students to Assist with Follow-Up

This strategy is appropriate for secondary education: 12 through 18+ years old. The rationale behind this letter is student accountability. A student always knows how to find me to get assistance. This approach encourages students to self-advocate.

Monday, September 14, 2016

To:_____

From: Mrs. Fitzell, Student Services Department

Hello! I have chosen to be your case manager for this school year. I am looking forward to be working with you. I am giving you a copy of my class schedule so that you may know where I can be found if you need me for anything during the school day. Please keep this somewhere in your notebook, folder, or your backpack. If there are any changes, I will let you know. If you find you are having problems with class work, I will be happy to find a way to help you or get you the help you need. <u>Just try to let me know when you will need me.</u>

Mrs. Fitzell's Schedule

BEFORE SCHOOL:	ROOM145B
A PERIOD:	ROOM 145B or Student Services Office
B PERIOD:	ROOM 176
C PERIOD:	ROOM 176
D PERIOD:	ROOM M1
E PERIOD:	LUNCH/ROOM 145B or Student Services Office
F PERIOD:	USUALLY ROOM 145B or Student Services Office
G PERIOD:	ROOM 202
H PERIOD:	ROOM 301
AFTER SCHOOL:	ROOM 145B

Sample Letter to Teachers to Assist with Follow-Up

A special educator may struggle to keep up with how students are performing in general education classes, especially if those classes are not co-taught. A letter similar to this one might be sent to teachers periodically in order to get feedback on individual students. Be careful not to inundate the general education teacher with too many of these all at once, or too often.

Date:

Dear _____,

_____is in your pd.
_____ class,

and has Academic Support Lab _____ period. Please take a moment to fill out the information below. This will assist us greatly in helping this student to be successful
in your class.

Please Circle One:

1. **Estimate Grade:**   A   B   C   D   F

2. **Turns in Homework:**   Always   Sometimes   Never

3. **Tests/Quizzes:**   High   Average   Low   Failing

4. **Do you feel this student could benefit from any ongoing support and/or Specially Designed Instruction?**
   If yes, please explain.

5. **Please list any assignments/tests that need to be made up/completed.**

Thank you for taking the time to complete this form!

Sincerely,

"Quick Form" Letter to Teachers to Assist with Follow-Up

This form allows a general education teacher to provide feedback on one form rather than many. List student names alphabetically so that teachers can align the list with the grade book.

Dear _____,

The following students are in your pd. _____ class and have Academic Support Lab. Please take a moment to fill out the information below. This will assist us greatly in helping these students to be successful in your class.

Return to _____ by _____.

Student Name	Est. Grade	Missing Homework?	Missing Tests/Quizzes	Assignments/Tests that need to be made up or completed	Comments

Class List Adaptations Chart

I was a high school special education teacher when I started co-teaching. Consequently, I was often co-teaching with two to three teachers in the course of the day. Class sizes ranged from 25 to 32 students per class period. In each classroom, we might have up to thirteen students on an IEP. We would review the IEP in August before students arrived, however, trying to remember 45 to 65 student IEP's was impossible.

To ensure that we were meeting the needs of our students, I developed this class list adaptations chart as a cheat sheet so that we could quickly look at a class of students and know exactly what they needed on a daily basis. It worked beautifully.

Here are some important points regarding this chart.

1. At the top of the chart, in the row across each column, put a code for each student in the class who is on an IEP, 504 plan, RTI plan, etc. You might also put the student' initials if you feel that the initials would not identify specific students to anyone but you. The key is to use a naming system that does not identify the student. If this chart was found by someone who did not have the right to know that students' information, it would be a confidentiality violation.
2. After reading the IEP, check the items that apply to each specific student. The downloadable forms available to you through the download link provided at the beginning and at the end of this book are customizable. By using the downloadable forms, you can create checklists that are specific to your students.
3. A data collection option is to put a date in the checkbox so that there is a record of any adaptations or accommodations that have been made for specific students and which day they were provided.

Now, when giving a test, the teacher or specialist can look at this list and quickly identify students who need extra time, an oral test, or a modified test.

The sample on the next page, is an example of the type of form that will be available to you in the download collection offered to you as a supplement to this book.

Adaptations and Learning Profile - One Page View

						☾ Student Initials/⏻ Information
						Tests: Retake
						Tests: Extra Time
						Tests: Oral
						Tests: Modified
						Tests: Scribe
						Write Assignments on Board
						Monitor Assignment Notebook
						Break Down Assignments into Steps
						Provide Copies of Notes
						Substitute Hands-On for Written
						Substitute Oral for Written
						Seating Preference
						Allow Word Processor
						Allow Calculator
						Allow Text-to-Speech Software
						Allow Speech-to-Text Software
						Provide Advanced Organizer
						Needs One-on-One Assistance
						Visual Cues & Hands-on Critical
						Easily Overwhelmed
						Distractible
						Written Expression Weak
						Verbal Expression Weak
						Auditory Learner
						Visual Learner
						Kinesthetic Learner

Differentiated Planning – Lesson Planner Idea Jogger

There is so much to consider when lesson planning that I created a tool for teachers to use as a visual reminder of what to include in a typical lesson plan. Clearly, the form is not large enough to actually use it as a planner. Rather, it's a visual mind map to provoke ideas and provide reminders that will make lesson planning easier and take less time.

There space for quick notes on the form so it can be used as a notetaker while planning lessons or you could laminate it and keep it in your planning book or on r desk for when you're doing your lesson plans.

The planning mind map helps teachers remember all aspects of planning for a differentiated classroom. So, again, use it while you are planning to visually "cue" you into remembering what methods you might use to meet the needs of all learners in your classroom.

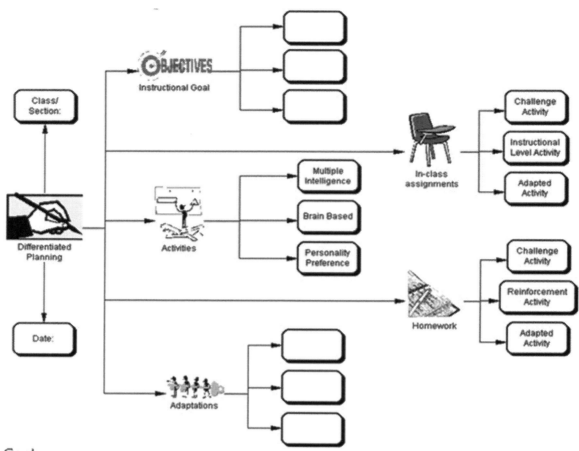

Goal:

Date	Activities	Adaptations	In-Class Assign	Homework

Assessment:

Know & Adjust the Reading Level of Text

Do You Know the Reading Level of Student Texts and Handouts?

I'm a firm believer that teachers need to know the reading level of the materials they use in the classroom. So often, the materials we use in our classrooms are much higher than the grade level we are teaching and, more importantly, higher than the reading level of our students.

Huge Discrepancies in Reading Levels

Recently, I've found huge discrepancies between Lexile scores, DRA's (Developmental Reading Assessment) and Readablity formulas such as Simple Measure of Gobbledygook (SMOG) and Fry. When I asked a reading specialist to explain the difference at a conference recently, she evaded the question by telling me (and the audience) to simply pick one and stick to that one. I disagree.

Awareness of Reading Levels is Important

If there are "years" differences between a Lexile score, a DRA and the Flesch/Flesch–Kincaid Readability formula, it is my opinion that we should be aware of all of them and question why there is a discrepancy. Why? Because they measure different things and consequently give clues to student reading ease or difficulty.

Choosing Appropriate Materials Using Reading Level as One Indicator

The varied formulas measure different aspects of reading, so therefore, they can't be compared. It's like comparing apples to oranges. Also, knowing the reading level of the materials we use with our students guides us in using text that is ability appropriate. Without this awareness, how can we choose appropriate texts for our students and meet their individual reading needs?

Readability Formulas

SMOG Readability Formula

The SMOG formula is a recommended and tested method for grading the readability of written materials. The method is quick, simple to use and particularly useful for shorter materials, e.g., a study's information pamphlet or consent form. To calculate the SMOG reading level, begin with the entire written work being assessed and follow these steps:

1. Count off ten consecutive sentences near the beginning, in the middle, and near the end of the text. If the text has fewer than 30 sentences, use as many as are provided.
2. Count the number of words containing three or more syllables (polysyllabic), including repetitions of the same word.
3. Look up the approximate grade level on the SMOG conversion table below:

Total Polysyllabic Word Count	Approximate Grade Level (+/- 1.5 Grades)
1-6	5
7-12	6
13-20	7
21-30	8
31-42	9
43-56	10
57-72	11
73-90	12
91-110	13
111-132	14
133-156	15
157-182	16
183-210	17
211-240	18

The website of G. Harry McLaughlin, who created the SMOG formula, can be found here: http://webpages.charter.net/ghal/SMOG.htm. The site includes a SMOG calculator.

When using the SMOG formula:

- A sentence is defined as a string of words punctuated with a period, an exclamation mark, or a question mark. Consider long sentences with a semi-colon as two sentences.
- Hyphenated words are considered as one word.
- Numbers, which are written, should be counted. If written in numeric form, they should be pronounced to determine if they are polysyllabic.
- Proper nouns, if polysyllabic, should be counted.
- Abbreviations should be read as though unabbreviated to determine if they are polysyllabic. However, abbreviations should be avoided unless commonly known.

If the written piece being graded is shorter than 30 sentences, approach it as follows:

- Count all of the polysyllabic words in the piece.
- Count the number of sentences.
- Find the average number of polysyllabic words per sentence, i.e.:

$$\text{Average} = \frac{\text{Total \# of polysyllabic words}}{\text{Total \# of sentences}}$$

- Multiply that average by the average number of sentences short of 30.
- Add that figure on to the total number of polysyllabic words.
- Compare the number of polysyllabic words in the SMOG conversion table.

Fry Readability Formula See:

http://www.readabilityformulas.com/

Readability Statistics in MSWord

In order to ensure that homework directions, quizzes, and tests are at an appropriate level for all of your students, MSWord can analyze your document to let you know the grade level at which you are writing. Students can also use these readability statistics to evaluate their writing and challenge themselves to write at a higher level!

To display readability statistics in MSWord:
1. Click the **File** tab, and then click **Options**.
2. Click Proofing.
3. Under When correcting spelling and grammar in Word, make sure the Check grammar with spelling check box is selected.
4. Select Show readability statistics.

After you enable this feature, open a file that you want to check, and **check the spelling**. When Outlook or Word finishes checking the spelling and grammar, it displays information about the reading level of the document.

IMPORTANT: Do not include word banks or word lists in readability checks. They skew the score and yield inaccurate results. Highlight sentences or paragraphs separately instead.

Acknowledgment
Dr. Mary S. Neumann, DHAP, NCHSTP, "Developing Effective Educational Print Materials"

To Reduce Reading Difficulty:
1. Shorten sentences.
2. Choose words that have less than three syllables to convey the same meaning as a multi-syllabic word.

AutoSummarize

Use AutoSummarize to highlight key points, create an abstract or a summary of a student's writing. Use it to summarize information that is too long for some students to read. Use the following resource

For the AutoSummarize Resources See:

http://www.summarizethis.com/
https://www.tools4noobs.com/summarize/
http://smmry.com/
http://freesummarizer.com

Chapter 5 Review & Discussion Questions

1. After reviewing the information on conflict resolution and bully prevention in this chapter, how might you utilize the tools and ideas outlined to promote a caring, inclusive environment your classroom?
2. What is your plan for modeling and reinforcing social skills and a positive culture in your classroom?
3. How will you provide timely and meaningful feedback of inappropriate behavior?

Practical Application

Identify and record one concrete example of how you applied the principles, ideas, and strategies outlined in this chapter to foster a more caring community in your classroom or on your campus.

✄ **CHAPTER 6** ✄

Lesson Planning Productivity Strategy

Chunking Lesson Plans™

The concept of Chunking Lesson Plans™ is brand new. I began to develop this idea early in 2012 after working with real teachers, in real classrooms, and seeing how they struggled to do everything that needed to be done in the time they had. For the purposes of this explanation, let's use the concept of genre as a topic example to explain how chunking lesson plans works.

If I have five on-grade level capable students with no learning disabilities in a small group, and I want to teach them the concept of genre — not to be experts on it, but to know what genre is and be able to identify three types — most teachers would agree that I could teach the concept in about ten minutes to those five capable students.

But here's what I see happening in classrooms:
You teach those ten minutes. Then you look around the room and you see a glazed look in Jessica's eyes, and David is kind of looking at you, puzzled, and you know that Rob (who is on an IEP) is just kind of "out there" at this point. So you go through a few more examples. And you keep asking questions to try and pull information from your students and get them to participate. It's like pulling teeth because the same kids are answering all the time, right?

By now 20 minutes of class time has gone by and you're still direct teaching. Maybe you've even included drama and visuals and you're doing outstanding direct teaching. Despite your best efforts, you realize that Rob might need a couple more examples before maybe, just maybe, he'll get it. So you go through another couple of examples that are easier and clearer and you're hoping he'll come along. Now you've spent 25 minutes in a direct teach. If you've got a 45-minute class, that gives you only 20 minutes for practice activities or whatever else you have to get done.

Now, what were those five capable students who got the information and understood it after the first ten minutes doing while you spent an additional 15 minutes going over the material again and again for the rest of the class? Probably going, "Oh, geez. I'm bored." Who knows, they may have even begun to act out their boredom and frustration.

Most of us would agree that after 25 minutes there's probably still a good amount of the class who are going to need quite a bit more practice and, in most cases, there are probably still a handful of students who have no clue what genre is. Weren't we there after 10 minutes of direct teaching? Why did we spend 25 minutes only to be at the same place we were in ten minutes? What an epiphany this was for me!

What if we taught our core instruction – the concept of genre, for example – for ten minutes and then stopped. No matter how many glazed looks; we're done. What if we did something different? What if we chunked our lesson plans?

So let's say we have a 40-minute class:

Day 1:

1. Five minutes of class is warm up. After the warm up, you take ten minutes and do your core teach. You teach genre, diffusion, FOIL method – whatever it is – and you do it in ten minutes. Direct teach is a best practice technique, and ten minutes, done well, is powerful. You really zero in as if you were in a small group teaching those five capable students, but then you stop. In most cases, you've lost some kids after ten minutes and you probably won't make more gains doing a whole class direct teach anyway. Now you have 25 minutes left.

2. For ten minutes you put the kids in mixed ability groups. High-middle, middle-low, etc... In those mixed ability groups, they are going to practice. Maybe you give them an activity; for instance, give them samples of different kinds of genre and have them actually use and implement the information you just shared. They practice what you just did for ten minutes, in a mixed ability group, and then you stop. Ten minutes, we're done.

3. Now we have ten minutes left of class, so you take five minutes to pull the whole class back together.

4. Once you get the class back together, you spend five minutes asking questions, clarifying and addressing weaknesses <u>based on what you observed while the class was in their groups</u>. Five minutes.

5. You now have five minutes left to do a three-minute ticket to leave, exit card, or a three-minute assessment with just two or three questions that let students indicate whether they understand the information or not. With this information you'll know who needs a re-teach, who understands, and who doesn't.

6. Finally, with two minutes left of class, you conclude your lesson and assign do-able homework.

Day 2:

1. On day two, use those exit cards to determine three same ability groups. Maybe the five-minute warm up includes going over, in pairs, the do-able homework they did the night before.

2. Next, take five minutes to break the class up into same ability groups.

3. Then take ten minutes and, depending on your goal and what you want to cover, do a core re-teach or reinforcement with the group who needs the extra time and attention, while the other groups work on review or challenge activities. The "expert" group might do an extension activity, enrichment, or a web quest. The goal is for them to go deeper or have them come up with a skit, a chant, a memory strategy, and then have them teach the rest of the class because when they teach it, they learn it better. They'll appreciate the memory strategies when they get to college.

4. Spend ten minutes in same ability groups then pull the class back together for five minutes and do a direct teach Q & A or review of vocabulary – whatever you think that five minutes is best used for.

5. Now you have ten minutes for core teaching, based upon your goals and what you need to accomplish.

6. Finally, you do another ticket to leave followed by a couple of minutes assigning do-able homework and concluding the lesson. Why? Because you want to know if there are still some kids who need additional re-teach. There almost always will be, but now there should be fewer.

7. And the kids who needed acceleration? They accelerated. You're still covering the same core instruction you were supposed to cover; you're just doing it differently in a chunked lesson plan.

CHUNKING LESSON PLANS™ 40 Minute Class Period

Day 1

40 min left
- 5 minutes - Warm up activity

35 min left
- 10 minutes - core teach (as if teaching five capable students in a small group)

25 min left
- 10 minutes - Mixed ability groups (High w/middle, middle w/low) practice, implementation, reinforcement in MIXED ability groups (group size maximum of 4)

15 min left
- 5 minutes - Pull class together - Direct Teach Q & A, clarify, reinforce key concepts, through essential questions determine level of understanding

10min left
- 5 minutes - Exit Card - Assess each student's understanding and identify those who need re-teaching, those who need practice and those who need enrichment.

5 min left
- 5 minutes - re-arrange desks for next class, verify homework, time for questions, etc.

CHUNKING LESSON PLANS™
40 Minute Class Period

40 min left
- 5 minutes - Warm up activity - Students pair up and share homework results

35 min left
- 5 minutes - Provide instructions for group activity to follow - call out groups

30 min left
- 10 minutes - 3 same ability groups based on Exit Cards: Group 1: Intervention/Reteach), Group 2: Practice, Group 3: Acceleration Activity

20 min left
- 5 minutes - Pull class together - Direct Teach Q & A, clarify, reinforce key concepts, through essential questions determine level of understanding

15 min left
- 10 minutes - core teach (as if teaching five capable students in a small group)

5 min left
- 3 minutes - Exit Card - Assess each student's understanding and identify those who need re-teaching, those who need practice and those who need enrichment.

2 min left
- 2 minutes - re-arrange desks for next class, verify homework, time for questions, etc.

On the following pages, I have provided samples of actual lesson plans that were chunked during a co-planning meeting. Co-teachers brought the lesson to the coaching session and together we adjusted the timing to enable each component of the lesson plan to be presented in a short chunk. The goal is to keep chunks under 12 minutes.

Part of the discussion included deciding which parts of the lesson were absolutely necessary and which parts of the lesson could be replaced by a strategy or method that enhanced the lesson by differentiating instruction and their hope for supporting all students in reaching a higher level. Aspects of the lesson that did not provide the best use of instructional time were replaced with more effective methods.

I chose to include block scheduling lesson plans because they are longer than the 40 minutes that I described. In this way, you can see how lessons can be chunked for a very short amount of time as well as for longer class times, as available in a block schedule.

The challenge when working with block scheduling is figuring out when to include formative assessments and when to schedule same ability groups for providing SDI, practice, and enrichment.

It's possible that the first 40 minutes of an 80 minute chunk could be "day one" and the second 40 minutes of an 80 minute chunk could be "day two." Teachers could take five minutes at the end of the first 40 minute chunk to review exit tickets and determine who would be in the three ability groups.

I recommend that teachers start with this structure just two days a week. It's preferable that they be consecutive days. Avoid a Friday and Monday scenario because too much time falls between the initial instruction and the group instruction.

The third day is perfect for a more fluid structure. In this way, teachers could teach the third day's objective, but also reinforce, supplement, and dig deeper into lesson objectives that were presented on the first two days. Then, if you find that this structure is beneficial, simply start the process over.

Chunking Lesson Plan Template™

Class/Period/Standard_____

#Class Min	# Min Activity	Lesson Activity	Classroom Teacher	Specialist	Comment

Chunking Lesson Plan Sample Lesson™

Sample Lesson
Class/Period/Standard

#Class Min	# Min Activity	Lesson Activity	Classroom Teacher	Intervention Specialist (if available)	Other
80	30	Intervention group Enrichment group	Enrichment	Intervention	
50 left	5	Transition – Students take out notes	Support	Support	
45 left	5	Review the parts of the body of an essay	Direct Teach	Support & Collect Data	
40 left	5	Students highlight: 1) Hooks and Leads 2) Opinion Statements	Parallel teach Guide students through activity – intense teach	Parallel Teach Guide students through activity – intense teach	Two groups – Mixed ability HML
35 Left	5	Direct Teach (Whole class) Students share what they highlighted	Writing student input on board	Leading discussion	
30 left	12	Working on one to two paragraphs of the body	Floats between groups and asks essential questions – Documenting response. (Immediate feedback)	(Two paras in the room) plus intervention specialist – divide the class into small groups	Mixed ability
18 Left	3	Whole class check-in – depending on results of classroom teacher, teachers	Direct Teach	Support	

		group assessments, either take lesson up a level, validate they are on the right track, or do a re-teach			
15	7	Working on one to two paragraphs of the body	Floats between groups and asks essential questions – Documenting response. (Immediate feedback)	(Two paras in the room) plus intervention specialist – divide the class into small groups	
8	5	Power Grammar Power Vocabulary	Fun Activity/Video	Team teach	3x/week 2x/week
3	3	Exit Card – (Determine re-teach/accelerate)			

Chunking Lesson Plan Sample Lesson™

Class/Period/Standard

#Class Min	# Min Activity	Lesson Activity	Classroom Teacher	Additional Information	Other
80	10	Silent Reading	Support/Collect Data		
70	10	Reading log/check	Ditto		
60	7	Unit Opener - Introduction - goals, essential questions, setting expectations	Direct Teach		
53 Left	3	Breaking students into 3 small groups	Direct teach		
50	10	3 - each group has a poem to read - (adult read aloud) and determine meaning, pull out images, what is the story telling them about poetry	Ask essential questions, check for understanding - data collect		Mixed ability
40	10	Whole class report out - Discussion, sharing.	Facilitator- use data from observation to drive discussion		
30	10	3-4 groups, second poem to read and discuss. Highlighting/underlining key terms from questions that they should be looking for.	Ask essential questions, check for understanding - data collect		
20	10	Whole class report out - Discussion, sharing.	Facilitator- use data from observation to drive discussion		
10		Exit Card			

Chapter 6 Review & Discussion Questions

1. After reviewing this chapter, what ONE tool did you find most likely to be beneficial in your classroom today? Why?
2. What tool or idea might you adapt for use in your classroom to increase learning, reach more learning styles, and enhance your teaching? How will you employ this strategy?
3. For your subject area, which tool or strategy presented in the chapter is most likely to improve the acquisition of knowledge for all learners? How?

Practical Application

Using the tools and forms in this chapter for reference, adapt or develop a tool to promote and increase student success in your classroom or subject area.

⚗ CHAPTER 7 ⚗

Instructional Strategies That Promote Success

Science proves that when we teach to a variety of learning styles and vary our delivery techniques, we will reach more students consistently. But many of us still struggle with ways to accommodate those students who need additional support without singling them out in the inclusive setting.

The tools, techniques, and examples offered in this chapter allow us, as teachers, to provide accommodations that some students must have in ways that benefit other students as well. This is a win for everyone!

To put these strategies, accommodations and adaptations, into perspective, see how the following sample IEP pages apply the strategies to students with disabilities.

Sample IEP Accommodations & Adaptations

Following are examples of how to attach adaptations and modifications to the IEP.

Student Name: Dominic Seymour
Grade: 7
Auditory Processing, Sp. & Language
Case Coordinator: Susan Fitzell

Strengths
Avg. intelligence, athletic, working with hands, artistic, musically-inclined

Areas Where Student Will Experience Most Difficulty
- Word retrieval
- Limited vocabulary: sticks to words he can spell, limits vocab. use
- Communicating with adults and peers
- Remembering material presented through lecture
- Making connections
- Testing

Abstract Reasoning: Needs Concrete – Very Literal

Classroom Adaptations
- Provide word bank to use in short answer or fill-in-the-blank items
- Consider crosswords for testing and review
- Use/teach use of graphic organizers
- Allow extra time for response when asking a question
- Show models of material being taught, assignments required
- Use visual and graphic cues whenever possible
- Consider graphic organizers on tests
- Teach memorization strategies
- Encourage use of rap, chants, and music to commit material to memory
- When introducing ideas use clear, simple, concrete language
- Require that Dominic speak and write in complete sentences
- Work in small groups, encouraging Dominic to talk
- Use index cards to review sequential material
- Disregard mechanical errors when not learning mechanics
- Give Dominic the opportunity to correct mechanical errors before grading
- Encourage and provide opportunities for peer review and practice
- Teach new material in small chunks

Student Name: Mary Wiley
Grade: 9
Emotional/behavioral difficulty
Case Coordinator: Susan Fitzell

Strengths
Above average intelligence, energetic, outgoing, creative

Areas Where Student Will Experience Most Difficulty
- Transitions
- Adapting to different methods of classroom organization
- Adapting to different teacher styles
- Focusing on task
- Accepting boundaries for behavior
- Listening and attention skills
- Controlling reactions
- Picking up on facial expressions and body language

Classroom Adaptations
- Greet Mary as she enters the classroom
- Praise vs. Disapproval 3:1
- Have high expectations
- Cue her to refocus and get back on task
- Provide and/or help her set up organization checklists
- Mary responds best to a calm, structured, and authoritative discipline approach
- Use behavior plans with Mary when appropriate
- Establish eye contact when speaking with Mary
- Provide Mary with a warning/cue before transitions and change
- Use feelings poster when working one-on-one with Mary to discuss her emotions and the emotions of others
- Develop a close liaison with parents

Student Name: Betsy McClure
Grade: 10
Specific learning disability
Case Coordinator: Susan Fitzell

Strengths
Avg. intelligence, verbal reasoning skills, athletic ability, social skills

Areas Where Student Will Experience Most Difficulty
- Remembering spoken instructions
- Slow reading speed (reading at 4.8 grade level)
- Comprehending text/questions
- Reluctant to read aloud
- Research/study skills
- Spelling, handwriting
- Taking dictation, copying, particularly from board or PowerPoint presentation
- Organizing/structuring written work
- Lack of confidence and self-esteem

Classroom Adaptations
- Write down assignments, instructions (check readability level)
- Ask student to repeat instructions to you or to buddy
- Allow extra time to complete reading, tests, and class assignments
- Involve in one-on-one or small group instruction
- Use books on tape and lectures on tape
- Read aloud to the class/student
- Provide copy of notes, use buddy paper
- Encourage use of word processing software with auditory feedback
- Use organizers for research and study skills
- Use spelling tools: color, index cards, proofreader buddy, spell checker
- Use and teach use of graphic organizers
- Use/provide spacing guides: i.e., graph paper, vertical lines, darkened horizontal lines, etc
- Provide positive feedback: i.e., awards, notice achievement, effort

Student Name: Juan Diez
Grade: 11
Specific learning disability
Case Coordinator: Susan Fitzell

Strengths
Avg. intelligence, problem solving, athletic, social skills, persistent

Areas Where Student Will Experience Most Difficulty
- Organization of equipment and work
- Demonstrating real ability – poor tester
- Reading, especially at speed
- Remembering and following instructions
- Writing legibly, drawing proportioned diagrams, etc.
- Skips steps in math and science labs
- Self-image as poor learner
- Feels anxious, frustrated

Classroom Adaptations
- Write down assignments, instructions (check readability level)
- Use a calendar to record assignments or an assignment notebook and buddy review
- Use color-coded 'notes' (use highlighters, highlight tape, sticky notes)
- Teach organizational strategies: notebook system, classroom organizational systems
- Teach test taking strategies
- Allow extra time for reading, tests, and class assignments
- Adapt worksheets, tests, and quizzes using tools for following instructions: check box strategy
- Allow printing, word processing
- Provide templates for diagrams
- Allow 'safe' environment for testing
- Use organizers for research and study skills
- Use and teach use of graphic organizers
- Provide positive feedback: i.e., awards, notice achievement, effort
- Designate a special place in classroom to turn in schoolwork/homework

Student Name: Martine Fullero
Grade: 8
Visual processing
Case Coordinator: Susan Fitzell

Strengths
Strong math skills, spatial reasoning, creative, hard-working

Areas Where Student Will Experience Most Difficulty
- Reading average classroom print
- Reading hand-written passages
- Seeing/focusing on the interactive white board, PowerPoint presentation, or television
- Taking dictation
- Handwriting
- Copying, particularly from the board
- Drawing/interpreting maps, etc.
- Listening to lecture while copying notes

Classroom Adaptations
- Enlarge print
- Print or type when handwriting for screen presentation of notes
- Seat strategically – create a semi-circle or a U shape
- Color in maps, create texture maps
- Use audiobooks
- Provide a guided outline for note taking
- Use a device scanner app to copy notes for a student who struggles to take accurate notes
- Provide recorded lecture or allow the student to record lectures
- Encourage use of word processing software with auditory feedback
- Use one-on-one or small group instruction whenever possible
- Read aloud to the class/student
- Encourage use of Cliffs Notes
- Use and teach use of graphic organizers
- Use/provide spacing guides: i.e., graph paper, vertical lines, darkened horizontal lines, etc.

Difficulty/Adaptation Quick List

DIFFICULTY	ADAPTATION
Poor literacy skills	Provide simpler text/use peer support
Speech/language difficulty	Check understanding of key words Partner/group oral work
Listening/following instructions	Highlight/cure in to important information/provide lists
Poor numeric skills	Provide apparatus, e.g. counters, algebra manipulatives
Written work: copying notes, taking notes from lecture, etc.	Use alternative forms of recording
Grasping/retaining new concepts	Give more practice/use smaller steps/use alternative language/use memory strategies
Difficulty with maps/graphs/charts	Tracing photocopy – photocopy and enlarge, add color/shading
Short concentration span/keeping on task	Provide short tasks/frequent verbal cues
Distracts others/is distracted	Sit in front/isolate from others/explore supportive groups
Working independently	Pair with responsible partner
Keeping classroom code of conduct	Give positive reinforcement/diary of specific incidents
Relating to other pupils	Change seating positions or group/monitor triggers
Working in cooperation with others	Pair with responsible partner/define group roles
Relating positively to adults	Be a role model/negotiate one-to-one
Slow paced work	Realistic deadlines/allow extra time
Handwriting/presentation difficulties	Allow extra time and/or alternative ways of recording
Low self-esteem/lack of confidence	Notice positives/plan for success and achievement/give classroom responsibilities
Organizational skills	Encourage use of lists, routines, labels, study buddies
Homework	Time to explain homework in lesson/time for class to record assignment/use parental support
Becoming upset at difficulties	Notice positives/reassure

Adapting & Differentiating with Technology

Educational Videos

FOSTERING UNDERSTANDING THROUGH VIDEO CLIPS

Interweave your lesson with video clips that provide meaning and background for the topic being taught. Limit clips to 3-6 minutes.

APPS THAT CAPTURE AND PLAY VIDEO:

Video capture and video play have always proved challenging in the classroom. Given the uncertainty of buffering streaming video, blocked websites, and the inability to download or play certain file types, many teachers simply avoid video. Avoiding video is the least desirable option.

Imagine that you are reading a story where the storyline takes place primarily in coastal waters and island habitats. Your students live on a Navajo reservation in the middle of Arizona. None of your students have had the benefit of ever seeing or experiencing an ocean. Some may not even have electricity or television at home, and consequently may not have seen movies or television programs set around coastal waters. If this sounds outlandish to you, I assure you that this situation exists as I have personally worked in Navajo schools as a presenter and consultant.

If we cannot take students to the ocean, we can at least show them video that allows them to experience the environment virtually. Students will be better equipped to understand the intricacies of a storyline if they understand the setting. So much of the literature students read in the classroom has no connection to their experiences or daily lives. Video can create that connection.

Text-to-Speech Software

There are several speech-to-text options. One example is Balabolka, A text-to-speech application that uses the built-in voices of MS Windows to read text on screen or any text passage you insert into the program. This is a great tool to support struggling readers, auditory learners, and English language learners*

*Excerpted from *Use iPads and Other Cutting-Edge Technology to Strengthen your Instruction* by Susan Gingras Fitzell.

141

Speech-to-Text Software

SPEECH-TO-TEXT: IS IT STILL WRITING?

When most of us think about the skill of writing, we consider writing conventions such as punctuation, spelling, grammar, and other things that make writing consistent and easy to read. We think about sentence structure and paragraph formation. We think about organization. However, a piece of writing can have absolutely perfect writing convention and yet be uninteresting, unimportant, lacking passion, and void of analysis or reflection.

Before technology was an option for putting words to print for people who struggled with writing convention, only those who were able to do both the convention and the creation became authors. While some may believe that is only just, the bigger picture is that many brilliant minds, amazing storytellers, and passionate visionaries were never able to put their ideas into print.

Speech-to-text has changed that reality for those who struggle to put words to paper. Today, doctors, lawyers, business men and women, and authors are using speech-to-text. After speech-to-text captures their stories, their ideas, or their message, proofreaders and copy editors turn the piece into a respectable and publishable document. As a matter of fact, the words you are reading at this very moment are being spoken into a software program called Dragon Naturally Speaking.

In this digital age, it is not only appropriate, but possibly necessary, to teach students how to use these tools to maximize their literary potential.

Speech-recognition software, like Dragon NaturallySpeaking, allows individuals to input commands and data with ordinary speech. These programs must first be "trained" to recognize each user's voice. I have personally used this program to write the majority of my books. I could dictate into a phone or a computer while on an airplane, while driving, or while scanning reference material in my office. Then I simply converted it to text. With some editing afterwards, I had a book! Currently, it is one of the best and most powerful speech-to-text systems on the market.

Adapt the Format of Handouts, Tests, and Quizzes

- Add a chart or present information in chart format
- Provide information in small chunks - Keep facts on handouts and overheads to five to seven pieces of information with graphics (Furukawa, 1978; Lah, Saat, & Hassan, 2014)
- Provide models – Have samples of previously made projects
- Provide 3-D models of concepts being taught
- It is better to have white space on the page than too much material. What you save in paper, you lose in learning
- Add structure
- Present information in sequential order
- Use crosswords for review
- Reword
- Make the assignment hands-on
- Provide an outline
- Highlight key points
- Transfer word lists written on paper to index cards
- Lower the reading level
- Simplify wording
- De-clutter
- Add pictures or visual cues

Make Instructions Clear and Concrete

When I was co-teaching Biology, we would do a unit on Class Insecta. One of the projects was to collect and pin insects. (Yes, I know for some of you that just evoked an Ewwwww!) While pinning insects for their insect collection, some students needed to *see* the insect pinned as well as *hear* how to pin it.

This example is not professionally illustrated for this book. This is a deliberate choice. It's not necessary for teachers to be professional illustrators to use powerful strategies. Stick figures work very well and are more than enough to make a point clear.

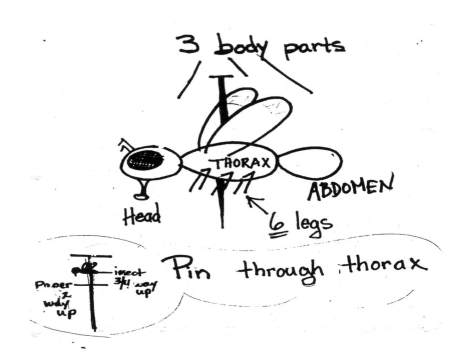

In social studies, one of my co-teaching colleagues realized that the reason students were mislabeling maps was because some students could not visually tell the difference between the land and the water. This could be caused by a Visual Spatial Processing Disorder. So, the co-teachers offered students an adapted map with the water colored in.

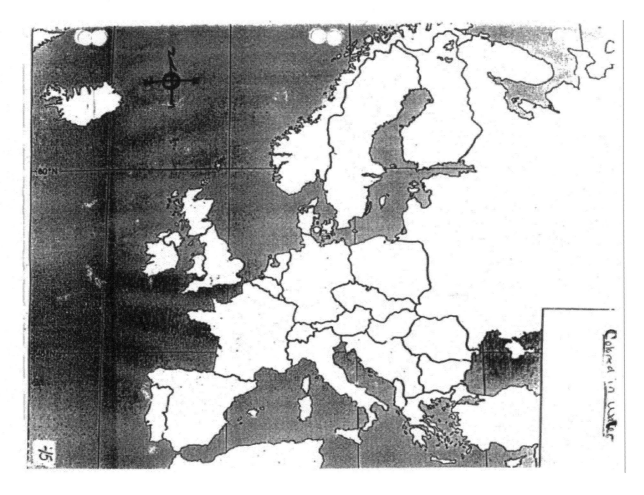

The example image has the water colored in so the land mass is spatially separate and different from the water.

Tips for Print & Screen Media

- Print it. Many students cannot read cursive well and consequently waste working memory space decoding the cursive, rather than taking in the information efficiently.
- Border key vocabulary, terminology, characters in a story, historical figures, etc. in the shape of the words. The brain remembers what's in a border. The border creates a shape and enhances visual recall.
- Printed text should be a minimum of fourteen points. Research studies have indicated that the larger font size increases student reading success(O'Brien, Mansfield, & Legge, 2005).
- The minimum font on a (Caine et al., n.d.) projection screen or an interactive whiteboard is 24 points. Anything smaller is too small for some students and adults to read on the screen. Also, we tend to put too much on the screen when the font size is smaller. The latest research indicates that the brain can only process 3-4 chunks of novel information at a time! After that, it's cognitive overload (Nelson Cowan, 2010; Farrington, 2011; Oberauer & Hein, 2012).
- Avoid fonts with serifs. They clutter up the visual field, making it more difficult for students with reading and vision disabilities to read efficiently.

Avoid Confusing Directions

Look for confusing directions in handouts, tests, and especially project descriptions. Even if unclear aspects are discussed in class, some students will miss the clarification. Provide the opportunity for success by ensuring the written instructions are very clear.

Often what is clear to us, because we know what we are talking about, is not necessarily clear to someone else. Imagine how confusing this is for the student with special needs!

- Look for confusing directions in ready-made handouts.
- On worksheets, put each specific instruction with the activity being instructed.
- Do not put all the instructions for one worksheet at the top of the page with two or three activities below it when each activity requires a different instruction.
- Use simple terminology in the instructions. Words with double meanings cause confusion. Some students will do poorly on a test or activity because they did not understand the language in the instructions.
- Break instructions down into bullets. Paragraph form invites the student to miss instructions.

- Provide examples whenever possible.
- When assigning projects, provide models of the completed project for kids to use as a guide. How often do we, as adults, need to see examples of resumes, letters, finished décor, constructed furniture, etc. before we can do it ourselves? Yet we routinely require students to create results from purely verbal instructions.

Below is an example of the progression from confusing directions that are difficult to see clearly, nevermind read, to understandable directions:

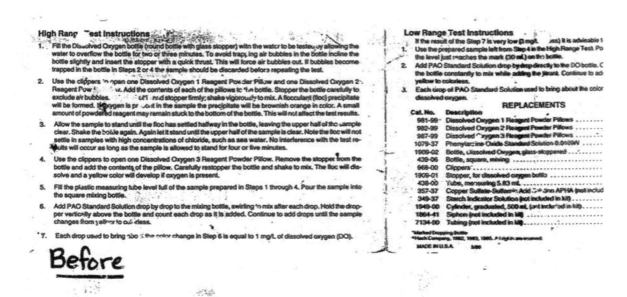

Although, you are looking at a "copy," the above directions were not much easier to read in the original text. I had trouble reading them!

So, given that my co-teacher and I didn't realize how difficult the directions would be to read until we opened up the test kits for the first time, we quickly brainstormed solutions.

We needed a quick adaptation, so hand writing the directions was the best option as a first solution. Done is better than perfect. The first re-write is pictured on the next page.

~~TITLE~~ ~~Identification~~

1. FILL D.O. BOTTLE w/ TESTING WATER
PUT STOPPER IN QUICKLY to keep air
from getting in. Quickly.
Let excess spill out.

2. ADD (1) REAGENT POWDER DO_2 (1)
(1) REAGEANT POWDER $D.O_2$ (2)
to Bottle

3. Hold stopper firmly & Shake

5. Let Sit 5 minutes = (brownish, orange flakes)

6. With upper half of sample clear,
Shake bottle again

7. Let sit 5 minutes

8. ADD (1) REAGENT POWDER $D.O_2$ (3),
to bottle.

9. Shake = (yellow floc)

10. Fill measuring tube level to top.

11. Pour into Square mixing bottle.

12. (count#) ADD PAO standard solution drop by drop
to mixing bottle & swirl after each drop,
until mixture is colorless. ? #drops ___

Second and final re-write is typed with a single image. Yes, this literally has all the instructions necessary and does not miss any of the steps listed in the first unreadable test kit instructions.

DISSOLVED OXYGEN TEST INSTRUCTIONS

1. **Fill D.O. bottle with testing water.
   Put stopper in QUICKLY to keep air from getting in.
   Let excess spill out.**

2. **ADD (1) REAGENT POWDER D.O.$_2$ (1)
   (1) REAGENT POWDER D.O.$_2$ (2)
   TO BOTTLE.**

3. **HOLD stopper firmly and shake.**

4. **Let sit 5 minutes = (brownish, orange flakes)**

5. **With upper half of sample clear, shake bottle
   again.**

6. **Let sit 5 minutes.**

7. **ADD (1) Reagent Powder D.O.$_2$ (3) to bottle.**

8. **Shake = (yellow floc)**

9. **Fill measuring tube level to top.**

10. **Pour into square mixing bottle.**

11. **(COUNT**) ADD PAO Standard solution drop by
    drop to mixing bottle and swirl after each drop,
    until mixture is colorless.
    _____?# drops.**

Clearly Define Expectations

All too often, when creating materials for students, we are not explicit enough in stating our expectations. I realized this when tutoring students and using another teacher's instructions. I often had questions about expectations and would have to go back to the teacher to ask for clarification. I learned that I had to, also, check my own instructions because I was guilty of the same lack of clarity.

Here's an example from my colleague, Barbara Mee, a Social Studies co-teacher, of very clearly stated expectations. She added, "No longer could students say they didn't know what they were supposed to do!"

PROJECT:

U.S. History 1   Time period: 1600-1750
Development of the THIRTEEN English Colonies and Three Major Regions

These are virtually the same directions that you copied into your notebooks in class...but for anyone who was absent, or might need to check exactly what my expectations are, you now have this copy. In addition, library dates, class work period, and due dates are listed.

1.   This is a group project.

2.   There are three groups in each class. (New England, Middle, and Southern)

3.   There will be three library days initially: October 19th, 20th, 21st.

4.   There will be class work and organization in the room October 25, 1999.

5.   Each group will present a poster, travel brochure or Power Point presentation that covers the requirements. Your job is to teach the class about your region.

6.   Each group must have a minimum of 8 sources. (You may hand in the library cards.)

7.   Each group must complete and hand in the "library" organization sheet.

Teacher clearly defines expectations

REQUIREMENTS (Check them off as you meet them.)

☐ Map with a minimum of 10 geographical features identified
☐ Government: What type colonies? (Corporate or character; royal; proprietary)
☐ Why were the colonies in your region founded? When and by whom?
☐ Religions and evidence of (or lack of) toleration
☐ Schools/Education
☐ Occupations and trade...How to make a living?
☐ Native Americans
☐ Climate and Crops
☐ Famous people
☐ Other: can include any interesting tidbits of information that you find

Checkboxes help students meet each requirement.

DUE DATES
New England Colonies: Monday, November 8, 1999
Middle Colonies: Tuesday, November 9, 1999
Southern Colonies: Wednesday, November 10, 1999

PLEASE NOTE: Each individual is required to hand in a self-evaluation. Details will be furnished to you.
Also: If you are absent on your scheduled presentation date, you will be given an alternate assignment...no exceptions.

QUESTIONS???????? You need to ask!!

Contributed by Barbara Mee

Provide Lines and Space

Following is an example of an assignment **formatted in a way that is difficult** for students with reading issues, organizational problems, or difficulty focusing to process efficiently and accurately.

ACTIVITY: SUSTAINABLE VS UNSUSTAINABLE ENVIRONMENT
PRE-ACTIVITY HOMEWORK ASSIGNMENT

For homework, each of you should find two articles. One article should explain one thing we can do to help make our environment sustainable; the other article should explain one thing that human beings are doing that is having a negative impact on the environment. As part of the assignment, complete the following questions on a separate sheet of paper.

You will be given several days to complete this assignment. It is important that you put a lot of effort into this assignment. The information you obtain on your own will be important to the success of your group when we use the information to complete a group activity in the near future.

1. Define the term sustainable.
2. Explain what you think a sustainable environment would look like.
3. Write an essay briefly describe the important points discussed in the article.
4. Most important: With the first article, describe why the activity being done helps make the environment sustainable. With the second article, describe why the activity being done is having a negative impact on the environment.

On the next page, you will see an example of how this activity may be adapted easily, allowing students to be more successful.

ADAPTED ASSIGNMENT EXAMPLE
(Note: Used Sans Serif Font & added lines and space)

"SUSTAINABLE VS UNSUSTAINABLE ENVIRONMENT" ACTIVITIES

Define, in your own words, the term SUSTAINABLE:

_____
_____
_____

After sharing your definition with your group, write the definition of SUSTAINABLE that the group has decided on:

_____
_____
_____

Describe what you think a SUSTAINABLE ENVIRONMENT would look like:

_____
_____
_____

ARTICLE # 1: (Explains something we can do to help make our environment sustainable.)

TITLE:
AUTHOR:
SOURCE:
SUMMARY OF ARTICLE:

ARTICLE #2: (Explains something that human beings are doing that has a negative impact on the environment.)

TITLE:
AUTHOR:
SOURCE:
SUMMARY OF ARTICLE: (Google Docs)

Students might also be given the option to use speech-to-text technology to complete the summary

Provide Checkboxes

Following is an example of a project description with and without checkboxes. From which would you prefer to work?

Not Adapted

Constellation Project

Introduction: The sky is an evening's entertainment. It is free and there for the viewing on any clear night. The night sky is alive with meteors, the planets, stars, and a vast gallery of imaginary figures – the constellations.

Once you know some of the many myths associated with the stars and constellations, the night sky becomes a splendid picture book brimming with adventures of mythical heroes, maidens, and monsters. With just a little practice, you will soon learn to find your way among the stars.

On a clear night, you can see about 1,500 stars with the unaided eye. These stars range in brightness and color. Seven-power binoculars will reveal a few thousand more stars than you can see with the unaided eye. Among the objects you can expect to see with binoculars are variable stars, couple stars, and galaxies far and beyond our own. Knowledge of the constellations will help you locate them.

Directions: Once you have been assigned a constellation, you will need to complete the following steps.

4. Look up the constellation in a book and draw the pattern of stars that make it up. Connect the star patterns with dashed lines. Please do this in black pen or pencil on plain white paper. You can even line up your pattern with a sketch of the imaginary figure it represents, but this is not necessary. The engraving should be no larger than a third of the paper. It will be cut out and mounted on black construction paper when it is done.
5. Look up a myth surrounding your constellation. Summarize the story in pen on plain white paper. This will be mounted on the bottom two-thirds of the black construction paper.
6. Identify the important stars in your drawing of the constellation and then describe each one by giving its magnitude, color temperature, and any other interesting information. In addition, identify how the star is classified: main sequence, white dwarf, or red giant.

After Adaptation

NAME_____PER_____DATE_____

CONSTELLATION PROJECT CHECKLIST

CHECK OFF EACH ITEM AS YOU COMPLETE IT!

1. ☐ Look up the constellation in a book. (There are books in the library and the science class.)
2. ☐ Draw the pattern of the stars that make it up.

> A. Use plain white paper.
> B. Use BLACK ink or pencil.
> C. Make it no LARGER than 3 ½" (height) X 8" (length).

3. ☐ Connect the star patterns with DASHED lines.
4. ☐ Cut out your constellations and mount it on BLACK construction paper at the TOP of the sheet.
5. ☐ Pierce PIN HOLES (not massive holes) through the stars.
6. ☐ Look up the myth about your constellation.
7. ☐ Write the story (myth) in YOUR OWN WORDS.
8. ☐ The final draft should be in PEN on plain WHITE PAPER.
9. ☐ State where the myth comes from.
10. ☐ Mount the myth BELOW your constellation on the black construction paper. (8 ½" X 11").
11. ☐ Identify the IMPORTANT stars in your drawing.
12. ☐ List these stars on the "IMPORTANT STAR CHART" (this is a special handout).
13. ☐ DESCRIBE AND RECORD in the chart the important stars, by giving:

> A. Magnitude
> B. Color
> C. Temperature
> D. Other interesting facts
> E. Classification (white dwarf, red giant, etc.)

Make Special Accommodations – Enlarge Print

CONSTELLATIONS

STEP 1

Constellations are groupings of stars. They are based upon the imagination of man. Ancient people gazed in wonder at the night sky. They noticed that certain stars seemed to form patterns. Ancient people saw these patterns as earthly things or as characters in their mythology. They gave them names such as Orion, Leo, Capricornus, and Ursa Major.

Stars in constellations are not related to each other scientifically. They are usually brighter and closer to the earth than most other stars.

Recognizing constellations, however, is important. They help astronomers pinpoint the locations of certain stars, nebulae, and galaxies. Ship captains, aircraft navigators, astronauts, desert caravans, and many other travelers have used them. Constellations and many of their stars are used to determine directions and one's location on earth.

People in the northern hemisphere look up at a different sky than those in the southern hemisphere. We use different constellations, nebulae, and galaxies than they do. Standing straight above the north geographical pole is the pole star. It is called Polaris. The earth is rotating directly under Polaris. Because of this, all northern constellations seem to revolve around Polaris once a day. That is why the Big Dipper may be found in a different location during the same night.

Constellations in the northern hemisphere close to the pole star are called circumpolar constellations. The most well-known ones are Ursa Major, Ursa Minor, Cepheus, Draco, and Cassiopeia. They are above the horizon during the year.

Step II
Here you will find a word search:

```
FUIOMHTRMVFDWLLIOPJDF
ASDFGHJKIUYNMLP4EWDDS
FUIOMHTRMVFDWLLIOPJDF
ASDFGHJKIUYNMLP4EWDDS
FUIOMHTRMVFDWLLIOPJDF
ASDFGHJKIUYNMLP4EWDDS
FUIOMHTRMVFDWLLIOPJDF
ASDFGHJKIUYNMLP4EWDDS
```

STEP 3
Answer an essay question on the following lines

_____

_____

_____

FINDING THE POLE STAR

Step 3

1. This section of the worksheet is a fill-in section that is very small with very small spaces to answer the questions.

2. This is the first question and the answer goes here _____. And that's all the room you get.

3. This is the second question and that's all the room you get because the answer goes here _____.

4. This is the _____ question and the answer goes here _____. And that's all the room you get.

5. This is the fourth question and the _____ goes here _____. And that's all the room you get.

6. This is the fifth question and the answer goes here _____. And that's all the _____ you get.

7. This is the sixth question and the answer goes here _____. And that's all the room you get.

8. Etc.

9. This is the first question and the answer goes here _____. And that's all the room you get.

10. This is the second question and that's all the room you get because the answer goes here _____.

11. This is the _____ question and the answer goes here _____. And that's all the room you get.

12. This is the fourth question and the _____ goes here _____. And that's all the room you get.

13. This is the fifth question and the answer goes here _____. And that's all the _____ you get.

14. This is the sixth question and the answer goes here _____. And that's all the room you get.

15. Etc.

This is NOT a real worksheet. This is a "visual" example.
The word search is not real.

Simply enlarge the text by photocopying, or if digital, selecting text with a small font and pasting it in a separate document. Then enlarge it. Print 5-10 copies depending on the size of your class and put them where students can get them on their own. Then announce that the enlarged copies exist for "anyone who may prefer to read a larger font size." There's no reason to call out students with reading difficulties.

CONSTELLATIONS

STEP 1

Constellations are groupings of stars. They are based upon the imagination of man. Ancient people gazed in wonder at the night sky. They noticed that certain stars seemed to form patterns. Ancient people saw these patterns as earthly things or as characters in their mythology. They gave them names such as Orion, Leo, Capricornus, and Ursa Major.

Stars in constellations are not related to each other scientifically. They are usually brighter and closer to the earth than most other stars.

Recognizing constellations, however, is important. They help astronomers pinpoint the locations of certain stars, nebulae, and galaxies. Ship captains, aircraft navigators, astronauts, desert caravans, and many other travelers have used them. Constellations and many of their stars are used to determine directions and one's location on earth.

People in the northern hemisphere look up at a different sky than those in the southern hemisphere. We use different constellations, nebulae, and galaxies than they do. Standing straight above the north geographical pole is the pole star. It is called Polaris. The earth is rotating directly under Polaris. Because of this, all northern constellations seem to revolve around Polaris once a day. That is why the Big Dipper may be found in a different location during the same night.

Constellations in the northern hemisphere close to the pole star are called circumpolar constellations. The most well-known ones are Ursa Major, Ursa Minor, Cepheus, Draco, and Cassiopeia. They are above the horizon during the year.

Provide Choices: Example - World History Report

ASSIGNMENT: NEWS PROJECT   DUE
DATE_____

CHOOSE ONE: Newspaper Reporter
                      Radio Commentator
                      TV Commentator

NEWSPAPER REPORTER: You are a reporter who has been given a special project. The time period is _____. You must choose your own topic (be specific) and write a feature article. As with any newspaper, the article must be well-written or the editor will not accept it, and you will not be paid (with a grade). You will be given one chance to rewrite it for credit.

It must be historically accurate and interesting to read. You must, in your article, establish why the event is important or will be important to historians and other people in the future.

BASIC SET-UP:

☐	a) Minimum of 1 full written page on stand.
☐	b) Must be set up to look like an actual newspaper article.
☐	c) Final copy in ink or typed.

REQUIREMENTS		DATE DUE
☐	Topic approved	
☐	Research completed	
☐	Final copy due	

RADIO OR TV COMMENTATOR: You are a radio news reporter (or TV reporter) who has been given a special project. The time period is _____. You must choose your own topic (be specific) and make a video or audio recording. As with any special radio (or TV) report, your recorded feature must be interesting and presented in a professional radio (or TV) manner. As always, the editor must approve the recorded program or you will not be paid (with a grade). A one-page fact sheet must be presented with your recording. You will be given one chance to re-record your news feature and re-write your fact sheet. It must be historically accurate and interesting to hear (or watch). You must, in your recording, establish why the event is important or will be important to the historians and other people in the future.

BASIC SET-UP:

☐	a) 1 page fact sheet must be handed in with the tape.
☐	b) News show must be presented like an actual radio (TV) news show.
☐	c) Final copy in ink or typed.

REQUIREMENTS		DATE DUE
☐	Topic approved	
☐	Research completed	
☐	Final copy due	

Math Tip for Visual Spatial Difficulties

Are you tired of seeing math problems all jumbled up on an unlined piece of paper? Does it cause students with spatial and organizational difficulties to make mistakes because numbers and equations are not lined up properly? Does it make correcting difficult? Here's a simple solution!

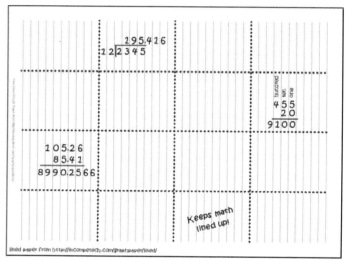

Keep math lined up! Turn standard lined paper sideways.
Grid paper also works very well. Make your own grid paper with enlarged grids.

Consider laminating dark lined grid paper. Students place the laminated grid under worksheets and workbook pages to line up their math!

For young children, use wide lined paper or paper with a large grid.

Half Sheet Theory[9]

The half sheet theory is very simple. Instead of putting homework problems on one side of one sheet of paper, put them on both sides of a half sheet of paper. Psychologically, students think they are only getting a half sheet of homework. Then if they complain about homework, you can say, "Ah, it's just a half sheet. Come on, you can do a half sheet of homework!"

It's a little more work to run problems on both sides of a paper and cut it down the middle, but, according to Annette Gorgoglione, a high school math teacher, it works!

Reduce to lowest terms

$\frac{10}{40}$ =	$\frac{8}{20}$ =	$\frac{40}{50}$ =	$\frac{9}{12}$ =	$\frac{5}{20}$ =
$\frac{20}{25}$ =	$\frac{4}{10}$ =	$\frac{4}{40}$ =	$\frac{10}{20}$ =	$\frac{4}{20}$ =
$\frac{2}{6}$ =	$\frac{15}{20}$ =	$\frac{3}{15}$ =	$\frac{12}{15}$ =	$\frac{20}{30}$ =
$\frac{30}{40}$ =	$\frac{6}{10}$ =	$\frac{3}{9}$ =	$\frac{2}{20}$ =	$\frac{20}{50}$ =
$\frac{3}{30}$ =	$\frac{6}{8}$ =	$\frac{6}{15}$ =	$\frac{3}{12}$ =	$\frac{12}{20}$ =
$\frac{4}{8}$ =	$\frac{2}{10}$ =	$\frac{10}{25}$ =	$\frac{2}{8}$ =	$\frac{5}{10}$ =
$\frac{10}{15}$ =	$\frac{15}{25}$ =	$\frac{4}{6}$ =	$\frac{8}{12}$ =	$\frac{5}{50}$ =
$\frac{8}{10}$ =	$\frac{10}{50}$ =	$\frac{3}{6}$ =	$\frac{10}{30}$ =	$\frac{6}{9}$ =

[9] Idea contributed by Annette Gorgoglione, Londonderry High School, Londonderry, NH

Tools & Techniques to Help Students Focus

Brain Gym® Brain Gymnastics: A Wakeup Call to the Brain[10]

Brain Gym is a series of exercises that enables the brain to work at its best. The techniques are a composite of many differing sciences based predominantly upon neurobiology. It has been found to facilitate learning in children with learning disabilities. However, the results of using Brain Gym have proven to be highly effective for all learners. There is even evidence that Brain Gym can be used for psychological disorders as well.

Teachers will find these exercises enhance student performance before test taking in particular, but also they work before listening to lectures and studying. Brain Gym also may relieve stress.

How does it work? Carla Hannaford, Ph.D., neurophysiologist, states in "Smart Moves" that our bodies are very much a part of all our learning, and learning is not an isolated "brain" function. Every nerve and cell is a network contributing to our intelligence and our learning capability. She states, "movement activates the neural wiring throughout the body, making the whole body the instrument of learning." Carla states that "sensation" forms the basis of concepts from which "thinking" evolves.

Brain Gym exercises consider our bi-cameral brain. The brain has a left and a right hemisphere, each one doing certain distinct tasks. Often, one side of our brain works more than the other, depending upon the tasks we are doing or how we have developed as human beings. If the two brains are working fully and sharing information across the Corpus Callosum, then there is a balance of brain function. Without this balance, there is always going to be something that is not understood or remembered. Brain Gym assists in integrating the two brains which gives us full capacity for problem solving or learning.

We are also "electrical" beings and our brain's neurons work by electrical connections. Water has been found to be the best thing we can do to facilitate the thinking process because of its capacity to conduct electricity and assist cell

---

[10] Adapted from an article by Ruth Trimble (trimble@hawaii.edu).

Much of the factual material for this section is taken from Smart Moves *by **Carla Hannaford, Ph.D.** and **Dr. Paul Dennison** and his Educational Kinesiology (Edu-K) literature. Please cite these authors when using this material. There are qualified Brain Gym Instructors all over the country; a link to Brain Gym online resources is given in the appendix. Permission to use my data is given, but it constitutes only my opinion and limited practical experience and is not in any way intended to represent the official Brain Gym or Edu-K view, nor give permission to reproduce the detailed exercises designed by the other authors without citing them.*

function. As Carla Hannaford says, "Water comprises more of the brain (with estimates of 90%) than of any other organ of the body." Thus, a simple drink of water before a test or before going to class can have a profound effect on our brain's readiness to work. Unfortunately, coffee or soda will have the opposite effect, since these will upset the electrolytes in the brain. In all, the exercises you see here are designed to make us whole-brain learners. Some simple but effective ways to wake up the brain and get it all working at once and optimally:

Before any of the following exercises, DRINK a glass of water.

"Hook Ups"

This works well for nerves before a test or special event such as making a speech. Anytime there is nervousness or anxiety, this will calm.

1. Sit for this activity and cross the right leg over the left at the ankles.
2. Take your right wrist and cross it over the left wrist and link up the fingers so that the right wrist is on top.
3. Now bend the elbows out and gently turn the fingers in toward the body until they rest on the sternum (breast bone) in the center of the chest.
4. Stay in this position.
5. Touch your tongue to your palate.
6. Breathe in through your nose and out through your mouth in slow, deep, belly breaths.
7. Keep the ankles crossed and the wrists crossed and then breathe evenly in this position for a few minutes.
8. You will be noticeably calmer after that time.

"Cross Crawl"

This exercise assists the corpus callosum (the tissue that connects the two brains) by forcing signals to pass between the brains and cross over the mid-point.
1. You can stand or sit for this. Put the right hand across the body to the left knee as you raise it, and then do the same thing for the left hand on the right knee just as if you were marching.
2. Just do this either sitting or standing for about two minutes.

Ruth Trimble states, "My student test scores have gone up because of Brain Gym. I have children achieving far higher scores than I have seen using the same screening and testing methods for the past six years. The ones who are doing Brain Gym are accomplishing so much more."

Mandalas as a Tool to Focus, Calm, and Get Creative

- Working from the center to the edge: Broadens attention
- Working from the edge to center: Focuses attention
- Relaxes the body
- Activates the right brain
- Visual prompt/structural map for writing feelings in a poem, song, or composition
- "Tilt the brain so language comes out differently" -Caryn Mirriam-Goldberg, author of *Write Where You Are* from Free Spirit Press

A source for mandalas can be found at http://www.mandali.com/.

Color Your Own Mandala

Sample from Monique Mandali, *Everyone's Mandala Coloring Book*,
<u>http://www.mandali.com/</u>

Interventions for Students with ADHD

Robert daydreamed so much that he was put out of school. Frank went into such trancelike dreams that one had to shout at him to bring him back. Equally problematic were Sam's restlessness and verbal diatribes. Virginia, too, demonstrated a tendency to talk on and on. Thomas experienced school problems, in part because of his high energy. Nick's tendency to act without thinking caused him to have several scrapes with death and near-tragedies, such as plunging to the earth from the roof of a barn, clutching an umbrella. In these examples we can see how the concentration, high energy, and unique ways of thinking and behaving that were exemplified by Robert Frost, Frank Lloyd Wright, Samuel Taylor Coleridge, Virginia Woolf, Thomas Edison, and Nikola Tesla resulted in school problems, dark diagnoses, or worse. These are examples of creative individuals whose behavior could also be interpreted as the inattention, impulsivity, and hyperactivity of Attention Deficit Hyperactivity Disorder.

--Bonnie Cramond, Ph.D., The University of Georgia, March 1995
http://borntoexplore.org/adhd.htm

The above link is the original source. It is no longer active.

Tips for Difficulty with Attention & Distractions

- Make use of **non-verbal signals** to cue student before transitions, or to stop all activity and focus on the teacher.
- Assign students **Task Buddies** to help keep partner on task.
- Seat students near the center of instruction.
- Seat distractible students surrounded by well-focused students.
- Use physical proximity to help cue student to return to task.
- Allow **quiet fidget toys, doodling, or mandalas** to help students focus. Fidget toys can include craft rings threaded with beads for calming.
- If students doodle, ask them to create doodles in the margins that illustrate their notes, enhancing visual recall. Later, ask them the paraphrase the meaning of their doodles.
- Clearly define expectations.
- **Vary tone of voice** when presenting to students. (If you can pull off a dramatic flair, it works well.)
- **Provide study carrels or partitions** to reduce visual distractions during seatwork or test taking as appropriate. (This should be a student choice, not a punishment.)
- **Provide sound-reducing headsets** for students to minimize auditory distractions.
- Silence the "pen tapper" with the sponge from a curler.
- When possible, engage students in unstructured, creative challenges.
- Color or highlight directions and important words on the assignment.
- During silent reading, consider allowing students to **sit on the floor** if they ask. Some students become amazingly focused when they carve out their own space on the floor or in a corner in the classroom.
- Allow students to ask buddies for clarification on seatwork.
- Significantly increase opportunities for active student involvement in the lesson and utilize questioning techniques that engage all students.
- Consider allowing ADHD students to "tutor" other students in areas of strength. This often brings out focused, caring behavior and encourages self-esteem.

A Solution for Students Who Rock Back and Fidget in Their Seats

Students who tip back on two legs of their chairs in class often are stimulating their brain with a rocking, vestibular-activating motion. They are trying to wake up their (brain's) vestibular system. While it is an unsafe activity, it happens to be good for the brain.

What can teachers do?

- ☐ Give students activities that let them move safely more often, like role-plays, skits, and stretching.
- ☐ Have students who chronically rock balance on a rocking board while doing worksheets on a podium. It helps them to concentrate and keeps them from fidgeting.
- ☐ Build a small under-desk version of a rocking board. Students sit at their desks with their feet on a rocking board underneath and it keeps them from rocking back in their chairs.

You can find detailed instructions here:
http://sawdustmaking.com/Foot%20Rest/footrest.html

Can't build the rocking board yourself? Just ask the teacher of a woodworking class within your district or at a local tech high school to build one.

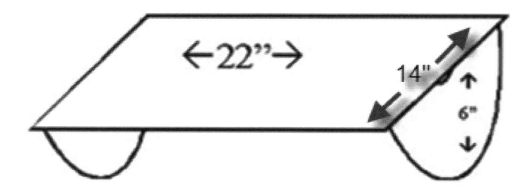

Interventions for Auditory Processing Difficulties

Follow the suggestions for ADD/ADHD. Students with auditory processing difficulties often exhibit the same or similar behaviors as students with ADHD. A speech therapist whose expertise was Central Auditory Processing Disorder (she had CAPD) shared that many students diagnosed with ADHD were actually CAPD, but rarely tested for it. Some vision difficulties also mimic ADHD.

☐ Supplement verbal presentation with visuals, color, graphics, and demonstrations.

☐ Allow time for processing information - **Slow down.**

☐ Increase amount of eye contact with students.

☐ **Follow the ten-second rule** before calling on students to respond to a question.

☐ Provide directions in **written as well as verbal** forms.

☐ If spelling is an issue, **allow a spell checker or text editor** to complete writing assignments.

☐ Keep **background noise in the classroom to a minimum** when lecturing or presenting information to the whole class. *Students with CAPD cannot process what they hear* when there is *background noise.* If possible, get a Sound Screen.

☐ **Monitor frequently** for student understanding.

☐ Write major points or content **outline on the board.**

☐ Offer many choices that involve creative expression.

☐ Provide an **outline or overview** of the lesson.

☐ Relate information to students' experience and background information.

☐ **Summarize key points** and let students know what is important for them to remember.

Tip to Maintain Attention While Reviewing Instructions

Put Prompts on Materials (or teach students to do it)

■ Simple prompts on materials can help students succeed.

 Star at the starting point.

Arrow to indicate direction.

START HERE ✓ Green mark to keep going

● **Bullets**

These prompts are presented in different colors. The simple act of picking up different color highlighters or markers works to keep students involved and attentive.

Considerations for Students in the Autistic Spectrum

Most of the strategies for students with ADHD and Auditory Processing Difficulties apply for students in the autistic spectrum. Following are some additional and specific considerations.

Communicating to the Student

- Be concrete and specific. Avoid using vague terms like later, maybe, or "Why did you do that?"
- Avoid idioms, double meanings, and sarcasm.
- Use gestures, modeling, and demonstrations with verbalization.
- Specifically engage attention visually, verbally, or physically.
- Use picture cues to communicate when possible.

Structure the Environment and Class Routine

- If necessary for understanding, break tasks down into smaller steps.
- Provide accurate, prior information about change and expectations. Minimize transitions.
- Offer consistent daily routine.
- Avoid surprises, prepare thoroughly and in advance for special activities, altered schedules, or other changes, regardless of how minimal.
- Talk through stressful situations or remove the student from the stressful situation.
- Allow for a 'safe space' in the building for the student to retreat to when necessary.
- Reduce distractions and sensory overloads, including noise, vision, and smell.
- Provide a designated work area. This could be a placemat on a desk.
- Label areas for materials the student will access or store.
- Provide a visually coded organization system for materials and notebooks.
- Post checklists and reminder cards to keep student on task and organized.
- Let student go a little earlier or later than the bell. Halls are a source of difficulty.
- Teach use of timer or other visual cues to manage behavior (Wright, 2011).

Presentation of Material

- Use visuals in teaching and learning materials.
- Use graphic organizers, charts, diagrams, and computer video clips.

Structured Teaching

The Treatment and Education of Autistic and related Communication-Handicapped Children (TEACCH) approach:

Structured teaching is an important priority because of the TEACCH research and experience that structure fits the "culture of autism" more effectively than any other techniques we have observed. Organizing the physical environment, developing schedules and work systems, making expectations clear and explicit, and using visual materials have been effective ways of developing skills and allowing people with autism to use these skills independently of direct adult prompting and cueing.

These priorities are especially important for students with autism who are frequently held back by their inability to work independently in a variety of situations. Structured teaching says nothing about where people with autism should be educated; this is a decision based on the skills and needs of each individual student. For more information, go to http://www.teacch.com.

Participation Strategies

Some students are less likely to volunteer to participate in class than others. You know your classes – some kids always have the answer (or at least they think they do), while others may not raise their hand to answer a question all year long. This is another aspect of personality types and learning styles that can be taken into account and addressed with a few simple tips for strategies that allow everyone equal opportunity to participate.

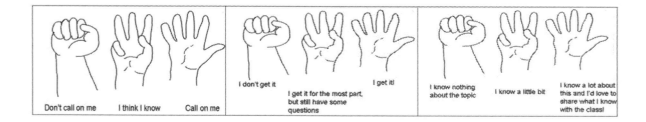

Use the Finger Count technique:

1 Ask a question and tell students you want all hands up in response. Holding up a hand with a closed fist means, "Don't call on me." A hand with three fingers up means, "I'll give it a try. Please help me with a clue and don't embarrass me if I get it wrong." Five fingers up means, "I got it! Please call on me and let me shine!"
2 Ask questions that don't require a right answer.

Choral Answers:

Have students answer questions as a "chorus" all together.

Individual White Boards

Use individual sized white boards to encourage participation:

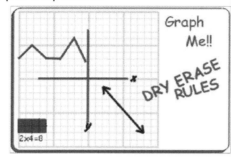

- a Every student has a:
    1) Whiteboard
    2) Dry-erase marker or wipe-off crayon
    3) Little kid sock (for wiping and storing marker or crayon)
- b Teacher asks a question.
- c Students write answers on white boards.
- d After fair amount of time, teacher asks students to hold up boards.
- e The teacher can see how ALL students are doing in one look across the room.

It stops blurters and allows those that need processing time to finally get it! (Rowe, 1986)

Vote with Your Feet

Another strategy that incorporates both class participation and movement — which we'll discuss later as a memory strategy — is "Vote with Your Feet." In this exercise, you give the class two or more options, which correspond to places in the classroom, and students "vote" for their option by going to the spot in the room for their choice.

Vote with Your Feet can be used in many different ways. Let's say you're teaching a history class and you're working on a unit about ancient Greece. You call the front of the classroom Athens and the back Sparta. Ask students to choose where they would live by moving to the side of the room that corresponds with their answer. Once they've made their choice, ask them why they decided to live there. Bonus points can be awarded for well thought-out answers — "Athens is a democracy and I could vote for the laws" would qualify; "My friend moved there" would not.

You can also use Vote with Your Feet to help older students think through their positions on complex issues. If you're discussing an ethical issue, such as capital punishment, you can designate one corner as "strongly agree" and the other as "strongly disagree." Ask students to stand in the corner that corresponds with their viewpoint; as an option, you can also allow them to stand anywhere on the line between the two corners if they don't have a firm opinion. (Depending on the issue, you may want to make it clear that their opinion itself doesn't matter for grading purposes — their ability to defend their position is what counts.) You can then ask questions, helping students learn by getting involved, putting their opinions into words, and defending their positions. Give students the opportunity to move between the two corners or further along the line as the debate continues.

All of these participation strategies are helpful when it comes to getting students involved who may not otherwise raise their hands; it may just be in their nature to keep to themselves, but their reticence could also be the result of limited English proficiency or the need for additional processing time. By having students answer all at once in one way or another, you can offer those that need a bit of additional time, the time they need and the confidence to raise their hands along with everyone else.

Note Taking Strategies

Cut and Paste Notes Using Mind Maps and Charts

Consider the graphic organizer on the following page and the different ways it can be used to differentiate:

1. Whenever you are presenting a "process," show the process visually in a process map. This will help the students to visually see what you are teaching and will enhance memory of the process.

2. Give students a process map or a graphic organizer with blank boxes and choose option a, b, or c below.

    a. Have students fill in the key words as you teach about the topic.

    b. Give students a grid of the key words, a glue stick, and scissors. Have them cut out the words.

        i. Then as you <u>teach</u> the lesson, instruct students to move the words to the correct box and paste them down.

        ii. Then as you <u>review</u> the lesson, instruct students to move the words to the correct box and paste them down.

        iii. <u>Power of Two</u>: Instruct students to work together to decide where the words go on the map and move the words to the correct box. Teacher might review student's answers and, when correct, instruct them to paste them down.

    c. The graphic organizer can be used as a quiz or test, thereby minimizing the difficulty for students who read below grade level. Students show what they know without being hindered by their reading disability.

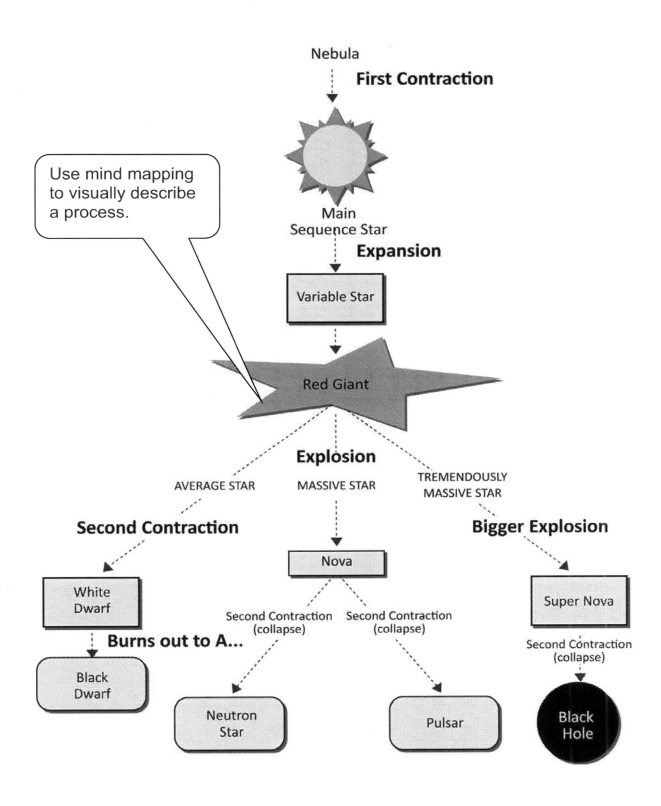

Sticky Note Method of Highlighting

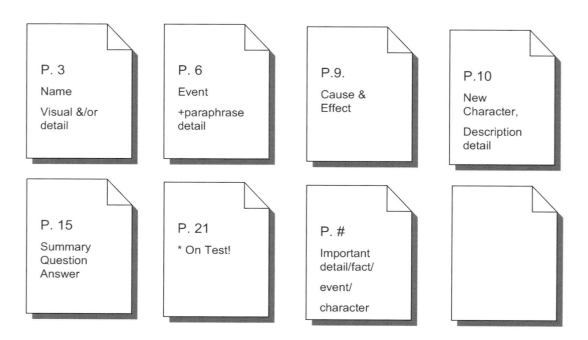

As students are reading a text, every time an important fact, item, cause and effect situation, etc., comes up, have students put a post-it note right in that spot and write the page number, the item and a visual or some detail.

1. After the chapter is read, the novel is finished, or the text section is done, students should take all the sticky notes and line them up sequentially (as in the picture above) on a sheet of 8 ½" X 11" paper.
2. Place the paper in a sleeve protector.
3. Students now have a study guide that ties into the text.

Landmark Notebook System

The Landmark Notebook System is designed to help you keep your papers, assignments, handouts, etc. organized and in a location where you can find them should you need to refer to them again. Like any new system, it requires practice and discipline until it becomes a habit.

You will need:
- [ ] One-inch binder. You can put up to two subjects in one binder. (Four subjects require two binders)
- [ ] Portable three-hole punch
- [ ] Zippered pouch with holes to fit in binder
- [ ] A ruler with three holes
- [ ] Eight section dividers per two-subject binder
- [ ] Two three-hole divider pockets
- [ ] Two highlighters of different colors
- [ ] Sticky notes
- [ ] Small package of skinny colored markers or gel pens
- [ ] Highlighter tape
- [ ] Pens and pencils
- [ ] Three column notepaper
- [ ] Three-hole reinforcers
- [ ] One accordion file for each subject in a binder
- [ ] Assignment calendar/notebook

To set up your binder, work from the front and arrange in the following order:
1. Three-hole punch
2. Ruler
3. Zippered pouch with highlighters, writing utensils, tape, reinforcers, etc.
4. Assignment calendar
5. Divider labeled HOMEWORK
6. Divider labeled NOTES
7. Divider labeled TESTS/QUIZZES
8. Divider labeled HANDOUTS
9. Pocket divider
10. Repeat dividers for second subject

Use sections for homework, notes, tests/quizzes, handouts for one lesson chapter/unit. When the unit is finished, move ALL the papers to your accordion file for that subject and label that section with the unit name. Save the accordion file at home for midterms and final exams. Do not throw study materials away!

For more information, contact Landmark Foundation @ 508-927-4440,
www.landmarkschool.org

Three Column Notes

Many teachers use a two-column note taking strategy when giving notes to students. However, a colleague of mine takes this up a level by adding an additional column. That third column is used for test questions.

Here's how it works:

The first column is for the big ideas, also known as the main ideas that a student needs to glean from a lecture, or their reading materials.

The second column is for details that support the big ideas. We might call this evidence, supporting information, references, etc.

In the third column, students reviewed the material in the first two columns and create test questions based on that information.

By creating test questions from the material written in the first two columns, students must not only comprehend the information but determine what's important. In a study based out of the University of Michigan's School of Dentistry, suggested that "student-driven, collaborative assessments can be an important tool for building critical thinking skills [...]" (Gonzalez-Cabezas, Anderson, Wright, & Fontana, 2015)

It takes skill to write a good question. So, another option would be for the teacher to go over potential questions with the students before the students write them down in the third column. For students to create a good question, they need to be able to key in on the important information and critical concepts. They might also need to understand relationships between different concepts in the notes(Gauthier, 2010)

When students create questions, there is also the opportunity for them to relate their questions to their own experiences. This then hooks that information into long-term memory because students are relating new knowledge with previous knowledge. (Arie van Deursen, 2016)

Take it up one more level: use only one side of the paper for the three column notes. Use the other side of the paper to illustrate the notes!

Three Column Note Paper

BIG IDEAS	DETAILS	TEST QUESTIONS

Forms that Provide Structure & Focus Attention to Task

One of my responsibilities as a teacher working with students with special needs and learning disabilities was to support their learning in our tutored study hall. We called it a study lab. Some schools call it a resource room.

A common practice in social studies classes was to have students read a current event and summarize it as a homework assignment. I realized that one of the reasons students had so much difficulty summarizing their current event was because they did not know how to organize the information. Also, they often couldn't determine what was necessary to cite. Consequently, they might forget to add the date, the source of the article, or even the author.

So, I created a current event form to simply structure the assignment for them. It made all the difference in the world for the students. Once they had the structure they found it easy to complete the assignment.

This was another one of those experiences where I realized that the reason that students may not do their homework was not because they did not want to but rather because they did not have the organizational skills to complete it.

The same logic follows with the Book Report Form and the Project Planning Chart. Once students had the structure and the lines and space to do the work, they could complete the assignment with much less difficulty, and often needed little to no additional support.

Current Events Form

Name & Date: _____

Circle one: World Nation Local

Do this: Find an article from a newspaper that is interesting to you. Answer the following questions about the article. Attach the article or a photocopy.

Cite your source: _____

Who is the story about? (Your answer could be a group of people, an organization, or one person). _____

What event or happening does the article tell about?

_____

_____

_____

_____

Where did this event happen? (A city, a state, a building, or an area).

_____

_____

When did the event reported in the article take place? (Time, a specific day or date, or a reference to a time – yesterday, last week, etc.).

_____

_____

Why did the event in the article happen? (Does your story explain what may have caused this to happen?)

_____

_____

What is your opinion about this article?

_____

_____

_____

Book Report Form

Title of Book: _____

Author:_____

Illustrator: _____

Publishing Co. & Place of Publication: _____

Copyright date: _____

Type of Story: (Mystery, historical fiction, science fiction, adventure, biography)

_____

TIME:
Historical period: (Medieval age, Victorian age, Early America, 1900s, etc.)

_____

Duration: (Over what period of time does the story take place? One day, several weeks, one hundred years, etc.?)

_____

PLACE:
Geographical location:

_____

Scenes: (Where does most of the story take place? Examples: outdoors, in someone's home, in a magician's castle)

_____

MAIN CHARACTER:

Name:

_____

Physical description: (What does he/she look like?)

_____

_____

Personality description: (What makes him/her special?)

_____

_____

How does this character change during the story?

_____

_____

_____

What feelings does he/she go through?

_____

_____

_____

THREE CONFLICTS IN THE STORY (The conflicts are the problems or hard decisions that the characters had to make.)

CONFLICTS/PROBLEMS	HOW DID YOUR CHARACTER DEAL WITH THE PROBLEMS?
1	

CONFLICTS/PROBLEMS	HOW DID YOUR CHARACTER DEAL WITH THE PROBLEMS?
2	

CONFLICTS/PROBLEMS	HOW DID YOUR CHARACTER DEAL WITH THE PROBLEMS?
3	

TELL SOME OF THE EXCITING THINGS THAT YOUR CHARACTER DID AND HOW HIS OR HER PERSONALITY MADE THESE PARTS EXCITING.

_____

_____

YOUR OPINION OF THIS STORY:

What did you like about it?

_____

_____

What didn't you like about it?

_____

Project Planning Chart

PROJECT PLANNING CHART

NAME: _____

💡 **Project Topic**   🕐 **Date Due**

I will present the project by doing...

_____ will proof read my project
(Hint: pick someone who can spell)

I will need the following materials

_____

_____

_____

I will look for information in the following places

_____

_____

_____

_____

Created with Inspiration Software

Reading Comprehension Strategy

English – Mapping it Out[11]

What is it?
This is a technique that helps students understand a sequence of events in a novel/story. It can also be used to help trace the development of a character throughout the arc of a story.

In what type of "classroom setting" can this be used?
I have used this with my English classes, which were all college preparatory high school students. ***Approximately 30% of my students had an IEP that would address their particular learning disabilities and modifications.*** This assignment was a successful learning tool for all of my students, regardless of ability.

In my classroom, students work in groups of four at large tables. They remain in these groups throughout a complete unit. In other words, when we began reading Charles Dickens' *A Tale of Two Cities*, students were moved into a new group of four and would remain with this group until the novel was completed.

When we read a novel, students each keep an individual reading journal. This journal is a place where each student keeps a record of her interaction with the text. The student records the sequence of events, copies down passages that interested/puzzled her, writes down any connections she makes to other texts, as well as any connection she makes between the text and herself. She also writes down any questions that occur to her when she reads.

Each day in class, students share with the group, as well as with the class as a whole, their reading journal entries. The class and group discussions are guided by questions that students wrote in their journals, as well as open-ended questions posed by me. The primary goal of my questions is to prompt students to return to their journals and the text to discover the answers for themselves. My role as the teacher is to be the person who provides tools for discovery. I do not want to be the person who spouts information that is simply copied down and then repeated verbatim on a test.

Telling students to "Map It Out"
When we encounter especially difficult part of the novel, I take out the crayons, markers, and newsprint. I give each group one piece of paper and an ample supply of crayons / markers. I then ask the students to map out the sequence of events in a specific part of the novel, such as Chapter 6. Each picture/image they create

---

[11] Copyright 2000 by Liz Juster, Londonderry High School. Reprinted with permission.

must be accompanied by a passage from the text. These groupings of images/text must be arranged in a sequence. Once the mapping is complete, each group will have to "read" their map to the class.

What special materials are needed?
- Crayons, art pencils, markers
- Newsprint or other type of large paper, preferably white

How much class time does this typically take?
Timing is related to the amount of text that students must "map out." The assignment typically takes one class period (45 min.) to map and one period to present to the other groups.

How is this assessed?
I will give each student credit equal to one homework assignment for the engagement in and completion of this project. This also allows me to meet, albeit briefly, with each student at the group table. I can then get an accurate understanding of who is doing their reading and completing their reading journals. I can also answer individual questions about the text.

A "Mapping It Out" Assignment for A Tale of Two Cities
Assignment (written on board and discussed): In the novel *A Tale of Two Cities*, Book the Second, Chapter 6 "Monseigneur in the Town" and Chapter 7 "Monseigneur in the Country", map out the events that happen to Monsieur the Marquis from the moment when he leaves the fancy party in the city until he arrives at his home in the country. You must have at least four events and a passage from the text to go with each event.

Vocabulary Building Strategies

Visual Vocabulary

What if we taught English vocabulary in the same way we teach world languages? Popular language learning programs teach vocabulary with visuals — meaningful pictures and other visual cues kids can easily relate to. Similar strategies can be very effective in the classroom when students are learning words and concepts that are new to them.

Several flashcard packages are available to help teach vocabulary using visuals. Vocabulary Cartoons, from New Monic Books, link vocabulary words with memorable cartoons and captions in order to reinforce understanding and memorization (http://www.vocabularycartoons.com). Philip Geer's *Picture These SAT Words in a Flash*, from Barron's Educational Series (available on Amazon.com), uses a similar approach. These sources both have SAT and ACT vocabulary, and Vocabulary Cartoons carries generic vocabulary programs for various grade levels.

I bought their flashcards, sorted through them, and actually found words I had never heard of. One of these was "antediluvian." I love the way it rolls off the tongue. But what does it mean? Antediluvian means prehistoric, ancient, and/or before the flood in the Bible.

The picture on the card is Auntie Lil is eating dill pickles and reading a book titled *Before the Flood*. The flood was ancient, and so is Auntie Lil. Remember this: *Auntie dill-lovin' lady is eating pickles and reading a book about very old times.* The pronunciation is "auntie-dill-luvian." You can see it in your head — Auntie Dill (pickle) Lovin' Lady. If you flip the card over, you see the definition and some sample sentences using the word.

Picture These SAT Words in a Flash vocabulary cards are somewhat similar. They have a picture on one side and analogies on the other side, along with antonyms, synonyms, and sentences.

These catchy visual connections work for many of our students. You might ask, "But what if our SAT test words aren't on the cards? What if I can't afford to buy them?" Thankfully, these flashcard sets aren't the only way to learn vocabulary with a visual connection.

Vocabulary Beyond Language Arts

Vocabulary in the content area is a critical aspect of a student's success in learning content outside the English and Language Arts classroom. This is especially true for English language learners (ELL). Research has shown that ELL students require up to seven to ten years of practice with academic language to become proficient. Not only is vocabulary as defined in the dictionary challenging for ELLs, figurative language provides an even greater challenge. These vocabulary challenges, also, impact students with language based disabilities. (Barrow, 2014; Kriston, 2016)

A student attending school in Boston might become, very confused when a friend exclaims, "Wow! That's wicked fun!" Wicked, by definition, means evil, or morally wrong. However, in the Boston area, wicked means "totally awesome!"

In addition, academic words have multiple meanings. In math, for example, there are many words that reference the concept of addition. Many of those words have additional meanings.

For example, words for addition include:
- add
- plus
- and
- combine
- sum
- total of
- more than
- increased by
- greater than

Words for Subtraction Include:
- subtract
- minus
- less
- less than
- fewer
- decreased by
- difference
- lower
- take away

Research also indicates that students who have not had academic instruction in their native language are at a significant disadvantage when attempting to learn academic language outside their native tongue.

One of the most important steps to supporting students' vocabulary development is pre-teaching vocabulary. Strategically, drawing upon context clues and/or a student's native language to foster understanding of the meaning is also recommended.

Beyond the academic vocabulary, it's also critical to teach the words used in directions. So often, students perform poorly on tests because they don't understand the vocabulary of directions and consequently, respond incorrectly.

Apps as Tools for Vocabulary Instruction

Cartoon Apps

The Internet, and the App Store, contain a variety of vocabulary cartoon apps that can be used in the classroom to teach your students new words. The more interesting the cartoon, the more the student will remember the word and even learn to incorporate that word into everyday sentences. This may even encourage them to write stories of their own using their vocabulary words (This would be a great time to introduce another type of app to teach writing – books and comics.).(Kriston, 2016)

MakeBeliefsComix.com is one example of an easy to use browser based comic strip maker. Comic strips are an outstanding way for students to illustrate their understanding of vocabulary words, demonstrate understanding of a storyline, illustrate a short story by converting it to a comic strip, demonstrate understanding of literary elements, figurative language, and so on and so forth. Students might use two frames to form pictures to connect to vocabulary for visual vocabulary flash cards.

Try http://www.makebeliefscomix.com, a site with wonderful tools for teachers and students alike.

Strip Designer is an example of a comic strip maker that enables the user to add visuals from a personal library and edit the design. Photos can be added from the camera, your photo-album, or downloaded directly from your Facebook account. You can apply filters to photos and change the layout of the page to fit your needs. You can even paint on the photos or draw your own sketches from scratch. Use comic strip makers and drawing apps to incorporate technology into research-based practice: Nonlinguistic representation.

Multimedia Tools

Research has shown a significant increase in vocabulary acquisition when students study language via Content Acquisition Podcasts (CAP) (Kennedy, Romig, & Rodgers, 2015)and other multimedia tools(Kennedy, M.J., Thomas, C.N.,

Meyer,J.P., Alves, K.D., Lloyd, 2014). Combining, video, audio, and meaningful images support language learning. These tools can be used both from a viewer and creator standpoint. Consider using screencasting tools in vocabulary instruction.

With interactive whiteboard and screen casting tools:

Teachers can

- import PowerPoint presentations, PDF files, and other documents.
- add animation.
- annotate and narrate the documents imported into the app creating a teacher-made tutorial.
- share teacher-made creations with students for whole class instruction or individualized instruction, as well as flipped classroom.
- record Lessons.
- create demonstrations.
- export videos to a teacher or student blog to support instruction, or directly to Edmodo.

Students can

- create their own video tutorials for what they've learned in the classroom.
- reinforce lessons taught in the classroom outside of class.
- create videos that can be used for assessment - and it's FUN![12]

Vocabulary Practice: Do-Able Homework

Why not have the students make their own cards? What if you say to the class, "Okay, we have 20 words to do this week — I'll give you some fun homework that you can do in several different ways. If you have a computer and Internet access, go to Google or MSN or Yahoo Images, type in the word *antediluvian*, and you will get some pictures as results. Pick the picture that you think means 'very old,' print it, cut it out, and glue it on a card. Write a silly sentence under it to help remember *antediluvian*, and write the definition on the back. Then bring the card back to class."

Divide your class into four groups. Assign each group five words. With five to eight kids working on five words, you should get at least one really good picture from the group for each word. If your students don't have access to the Internet, let them get creative! They can draw the picture or use the "Paint" program on the computer (Even the oldest computers have a rudimentary Microsoft Paint program.). Magazines or newspapers could be another source for pictures. Most

---

[12] Excerpted from 100+ Tech Ideas for Teaching English and Language Arts: Maximize iPad, Mobile and Online Apps in Every Classroom

kids now have access to a digital camera or camera phone. Could they take a picture for their vocabulary word? When they bring in their flashcards, let the students pick the best ones. Then you can scan or photocopy them and make more copies for use in the future. Brilliant!

Just one note: If kids are going to look up words on the Internet, parents should be advised to set the computer to *Moderate Safe Search* in Google Images so they don't get any unwanted surprises. I'm amazed at what comes up with some very innocent words.

As you work throughout the semester or year, build a file of these flashcards. This way, your students can use the file of flashcards to study for mid-term or final exams. You may find some handy uses for them in the future, as well — perhaps as communication tools for students with special needs or as a way to help a student who is out of class catch up quickly.

Visual Vocabulary Practice Instructions

Find a picture to represent a word on the vocabulary list.

Online picture database	Hand draw the picture	Cut and paste from a magazine or newspaper	Create with a computer graphics program such as MSPaint

Draw, print, or paste the picture on a 4x6 index card.

Think of a silly sentence or rhyme to help you remember the vocabulary word. Write your mnemonic under the picture. (A mnemonic is a memory strategy.)

Write the definition on the back of the card.

Write an antonym and synonym under the definition. Don't forget to label which is the antonym and which is the synonym.

Vocabulary Word Wall

Now that you have all of the words and pictures, make a "Vocabulary Word Wall." We often do this in lower elementary classrooms, but we stop there. Why not do it in geometry or algebra, history or language arts or eighth-grade English? If you're not allowed to put things on the walls, find a spot on a bulletin board, a whiteboard, or on the door.

Vocabulary Detective

The brain tunes out what becomes normal or usual. If you just post the flashcards on the wall, your students will get used to them, never looking at them again after the first day or so. To combat this, challenge your students to be "word detectives." Tell your class that every day, you'll be changing a few pictures on the Word Wall, and the students who find the changes will get a point, ticket, etc. — whatever you use as your reward system. Now every day they'll rush in to find what's changed, and they'll be actively engaged with reviewing the words on a daily basis.

Some of these strategies may seem geared toward younger students, but some were designed specifically for high school students. Teachers tell me this works, so why not? As long as you have a "caught-you-being-good" motivational system that works for their grade level and has a meaningful incentive, students will participate.

Vocabulary Word Bag – Five a Day

Here's an easy to implement tool that can work at any grade level. Anytime you find a new vocabulary word, write it on a slip of paper or an index card and put it in a bag. These could be words from your curriculum, from a story, from the SAT test, or just words you want your class to know. Every day, pull five words from the bag and put them on a board, with or without pictures. Tell your class, "Each time you use one of these words today in class in a question, an answer, or just a statement, I'll give you a point."

If John says to me, "Mrs. Fitzell, your outfit looks *antediluvian*," he earns a point.

"Mrs. Fitzell, that was a *phenomenal* lesson" earns a point. However, if Jane echoes, "Yeah, it is a *phenomenal* lesson," it's not a unique sentence. In order to get a point, the sentence must be original. Whether they get a point or not, the kids are still using the vocabulary in class, which is what I'm aiming for.

Sign Language

This is an interesting concept that deserves more research; I believe it could be very effective.

Parents are teaching babies to use sign language even before they are eight months old. If babies are communicating at this age, imagine what we could do with a bit of sign language in the classroom. This can even become a valuable skill to use in other life situations.

A fifth grade teacher told me one of her strategies for teaching vocabulary and spelling to her students. She handed out copies of the sign alphabet – the sign for each letter of the alphabet – then divided the kids into two groups and gave each group five vocabulary words. Their homework was to learn how to fingerspell each of the words, then come back to class, pair up with someone from the other group, and teach each other. After just ten minutes of practice, each child knew how to fingerspell ten different words – not to mention learning a valuable life skill.

Parts of Speech: Color-Coded Grammar

Montessori and other learning systems use color schemes to teach parts of speech. Writing nouns in one color, verbs in another color, etc. engages students as they analyze what color each word should be, and color is a powerful memory tool.

I made up a code for high school students using a driving analogy. What do you do at a red light? You stop in *place*. A noun is a *place*, *person*, or *thing*, and using this analogy, nouns are represented in red. You *go* at a green light, and *go* is an *action word* (verb), so green is the color for verbs. I created a picture of a car at a traffic light – this association connects multiple concepts together, because memory relies on connections.

Now when students are writing sentences, they can practice the parts of speech by writing words in the corresponding colors. Red is for nouns, green is for verbs, pink is for adjectives, etc.

Get the "gel pens" with all the different colors if you can, or just use crayons or markers and write larger. However you do it, I strongly advocate using color as a learning and memory tool because the brain thinks in pictures and remembers things in colors. Who wants to go back to black and white TV? How exciting was it when color showed up on the front page of the newspaper? But what do we use most in the classroom? Black and white.

The brain remembers what is unique, and color makes things stand out and be unique. This is what we are looking for in teaching: associations and connections that will help our students remember what they've learned.

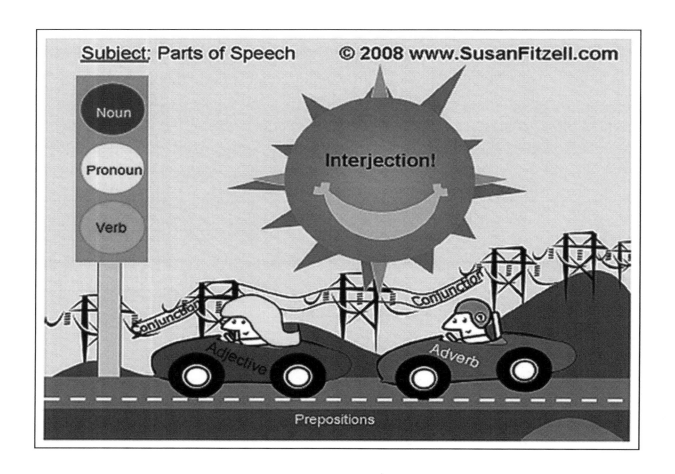

Writing Strategies

Breaking Reports Down to the Writing Process

I used the form on the next page to teach students how to summarize what they read. Plagiarism is a major problem for students with learning disabilities. Their intent is seldom to "steal"; rather, they simply do not know how to summarize.

The form breaks the process of research and summarization down into a step-by-step process. The key to student success is to go through this process several times a semester. I had them start a new one as soon as one was finished. We always had one in process. The other *very* important component of this process is teacher review, guidance, and instruction every step of the way. This process was painstakingly slow. I did a little of it in class every single day.

In order to help the students effectively, I had to read the articles they chose. I also had to help them summarize each paragraph in one sentence in the beginning. When each student is reading a different article, this is tough; however, I believed in what I was doing. The results were amazing. By the end of the semester, every single student in my class could take a standard magazine article, read it, and summarize it.

Tip:
Have the students choose more than one article. Students may pick articles that are way above their heads. It is important that they have a chance for success and an article from *The New Yorker* is probably not at the appropriate reading level for some of the students. Yes, I had students choose from that magazine! Use tact in explaining to students why they should use a 'different' article. This should not be a degrading exercise.

As an alternative, you can choose ten articles for the class and students can pick one of the ten. This is also more manageable for you.

English Paper Requirements that Get Results

NAME: _____ TODAY'S
DATE: _____

ENGLISH PAPER REQUIREMENTS   DUE DATE: _____

☐ Choose your topic:

My topic is: _____

☐ Use the library research, computer, or READER'S GUIDE to find an article.
☐ Attach 4 possible article listings from the Reader's Guide or computer printout.
☐ Choose 1 article.
The article must be longer than 1 full page of print and less than 3 full pages of print.

My choice is: Magazine_____

      Issue date: _____

      Article title: _____

      Page number(s): _____

      Author's name: _____

☐ ATTACH A COPY OF THE ARTICLE TO THIS SHEET!
☐ Write a 1 sentence summary of each paragraph in the article.

      Submit for proofing: Date_____ Teacher initials: _____

☐ Write a rough draft of your summary of the article AND include a paragraph stating YOUR THOUGHTS on the article.

      Submit for proofing: Date_____ Teacher initials: _____

☐ Write a final draft.

ITEM GRADED	POSSIBLE POINTS	EARNED POINTS
Reader's Guide Reference		
Copy of Article		
Paragraph Summary		
Rough Draft		
Final Draft		

Strategy for Getting "Un-Stuck" While Writing: Clustering

I can't even begin to count the amount of times that students would sit in study lab with pen or pencil staring at a paper unable to write that required introductory sentence. It seemed as if the phrase introductory sentence triggered writers block. I understood this on a personal level because I have never been able to write by beginning with the introductory sentence. Interestingly, when I have taken writing courses geared toward becoming an author, one of the first directions given is to just start writing, anywhere, anytime, anyplace. Just start writing. Never have I heard instructors say, "Okay, everyone write the introductory sentence of your book." Linear thinkers may work well with an outline and by starting at the beginning. Random thinkers, however, need to write ideas down as soon as they think them. Ideas must be captured before they are lost.

The clustering activity detailed on the following pages helps students who are struggling to write an essay, as well as young adults filling out college applications.

Clustering Activity Step One

- If your students have to write a paper, instruct them to draw a big circle on a piece of paper.
- Put the topic of the paper in the center of the circle. Note: If there is more than one topic, you might have more than one circle. For example, writing about three wishes will require three circles: one for each wish.
- Instruct the students to write any thoughts, ideas, and feelings about the topic in the circle. Students can also ask questions about the topic or draw pictures of ideas.
- Do not worry about spelling, grammar, sentences, etc. at this point. The purpose is to get the ideas out. Worry about writing rules later.

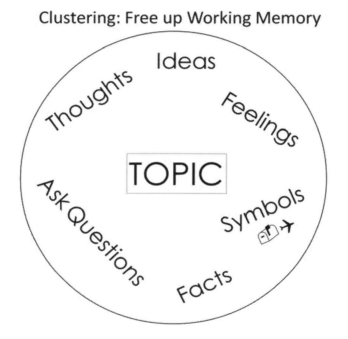

Clustering: Free up Working Memory

Make this circle BIG; at least the size of an 8" X 8" piece of paper.

- After students "create" in the circle, allow them to share what they have written with a partner.

Clustering- Step Two

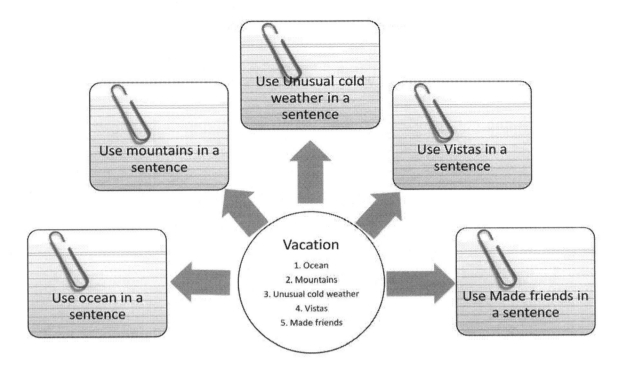

- Instruct students to take the "best" words and ideas from inside their circle and use each word in a sentence.
- This is the topic sentence for the paragraphs they will write.
- Write the sentences on strips of lined notepaper or lined sticky notes.

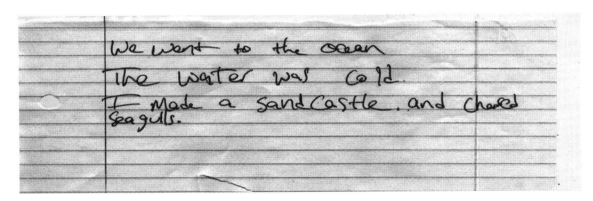

Clustering- Step Three

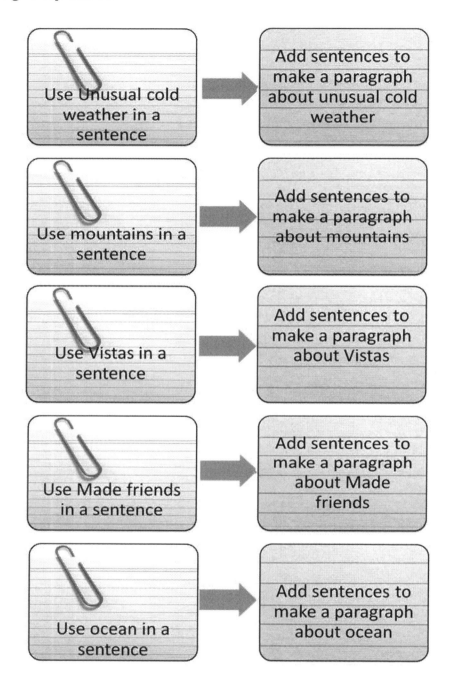

- Now, take each sentence and add some more sentences about the topic sentence on that strip of paper.
- Try to write two or three more sentences about the topic sentence.

*NOTE: Do not worry about spelling, grammar, or punctuation at this point in the exercise. Worrying about the rules makes it more difficult to be creative.

Clustering- Step Four

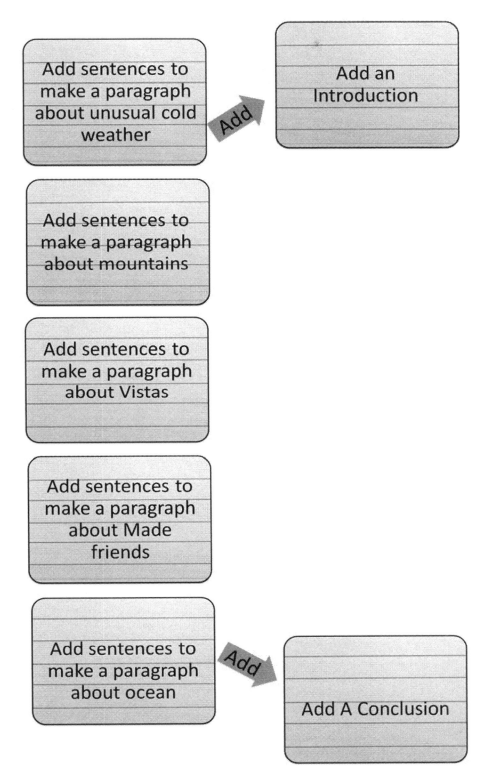

- Next, add an introduction and conclusion on separate strips of lined paper.

Clustering- Step Five

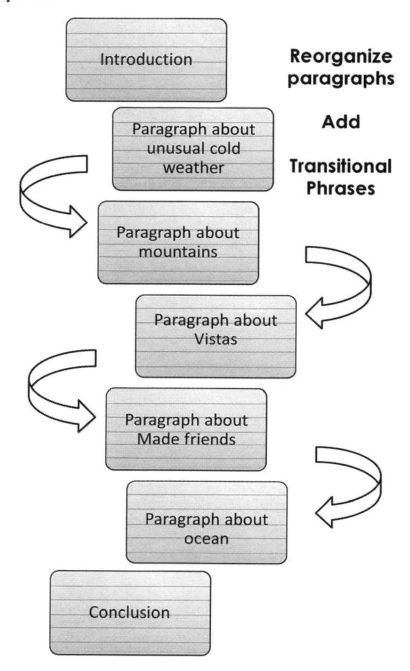

- Next, move the strips of paper around so that the paper is in the best order and makes the most sense.
- This process allows the writer to start anywhere in the paper. It frees up creative thought and encourages the process to start. Organizing the paper after paragraphs are written is easy.
- Tape all the strips on one or two big pieces of paper.
- Add transition words to make the paragraphs flow together.

Transition Words:

To Add:
And, again, and then, besides, equally important, finally, further, furthermore, nor, too, next, lastly, what's more, moreover, in addition, first (second, etc.)

To Compare:
Whereas, but, yet, on the other hand, however, nevertheless, on the other hand, on the contrary, by comparison, where, compared to, up against, balanced against, but, although, conversely, meanwhile, after all, in contrast, although this may be true

To Prove:
Because, for, since, for the same reason, obviously, evidently, furthermore, moreover, besides, indeed, in fact, in addition, in any case, that is

To Show Exception:
Yet, still, however, nevertheless, in spite of, despite, of course, once in a while, sometimes

To Show Time:
Immediately, thereafter, soon, after a few hours, finally, then, later, previously, formerly, first (second, etc.), next, and then

To Repeat:
In brief, as I have said, as I have noted, as has been noted

To Emphasize:
Definitely, extremely, obviously, in fact, indeed, in any case, absolutely, positively, naturally, surprisingly, always, forever, perennially, eternally, never, emphatically, unquestionably, without a doubt, certainly, undeniably, without reservation

To Show Sequence:
First, second, third, and so forth. A, B, C, and so forth. Next, then, following this, at this time, now, at this point, after, afterward, subsequently, finally, consequently, previously, before this, simultaneously, concurrently, thus, therefore, hence, next, and then, soon

To Give an Example:
For example, for instance, in this case, in another case, on this occasion, in this situation, take the case of, to demonstrate, to illustrate, as an illustration

To Summarize or Conclude:
In brief, on the whole, summing up, to conclude, in conclusion, as I have shown, as I have said, hence, therefore, accordingly, thus, as a result, consequently, on the whole

Clustering- Step Six

Introduction

Paragraph about Made friends

Paragraph about mountains

Paragraph about Vistas

Paragraph about ocean

Paragraph about unusual cold weather

Conclusion

Rewrite or type into one continuous draft on full sheets of paper.

Hand in draft for the teacher to correct.

If the teacher is not correcting a draft, parents may be able to help with this step. This is the time when the student uses the rules and makes sure that spelling, grammar, and punctuation are correct.

Clustering- Step Seven

Student writes final draft incorporating teacher corrections, feedback and edits

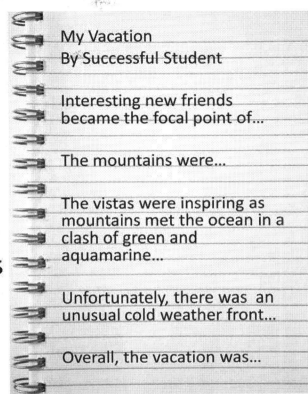

207

Ideas for Differentiating Instruction by Subject

Social Studies

- ☐ Decorate the classroom with students' drawings of the culture being studied.
- ☐ Make a historical comic strip that meets specific criteria.
- ☐ Compile a notebook of history jokes. Work facts into the jokes.
- ☐ Play charades with "significant" events from the unit you are studying.
- ☐ Create history raps that identify key dates and people.
- ☐ Play "What's my line?" or "Pictionary" with names, dates, places.
- ☐ Create time sequence charts with titles for major eras of history – then create a mnemonic out of the sequence of the titles.
- ☐ Write a skit or play from a period in history, or as a typical day in a specific culture. Example: Sparta or Athens.
- ☐ Make a game of predicting what will happen in several current event stories.
- ☐ Play "guess the culture" based on artifacts in a time capsule.
- ☐ Debate important issues and decisions from the past.
- ☐ Generate an illustration which best depicts what democracy* means to you. (Engages brain to store data.) *Example.
- ☐ Create limericks about important historical events.
- ☐ Make visual diagrams and flow charts of historical information.
- ☐ Have students conduct imaginary interviews with people from the past.
- ☐ Send a postcard from one historical character to another historical character.
- ☐ Have students draw a mural that reflects a specific time period.
- ☐ Role-play a conversation with an important historical figure.
- ☐ Make maps out of salt dough and show geographical features and key places.

English/Language Arts/World Language

- ☐ Teach "concept mapping" to help remember content or take notes.
- ☐ Create song rap to teach grammar and syntax.
- ☐ Write a sequel/next episode to a story or play.
- ☐ Use different kinds of music for different kinds of writing.
- ☐ Create crossword puzzles/word jumbles for vocabulary words.
- ☐ Analyze literature for "connections to our lives today."
- ☐ Practice impromptu speaking and writing.
- ☐ Predict what will happen next in a story or play.
- ☐ Experiment with joint story-writing – one starts then pass it on.
- ☐ Analyze a story and describe its message – reach a consensus.
- ☐ Use a "human graph" to see where a group stands on an issue.
- ☐ Analyze similarities and differences of various pieces of literature.
- ☐ Use a "story grid" for creative writing activities.
- ☐ Read poetry from different perspectives and in different moods.
- ☐ Play vocabulary words "Pictionary."
- ☐ Conduct language drill exercises with partner.
- ☐ Draw pictures of the different stages of a story you are reading.
- ☐ Write an autobiographical essay: My life to date, my life in the future.
- ☐ Use highlight markers to "colorize" parts of a story or poem. (Option: highlight tape.)
- ☐ Write a new poem each day of the week on "Who Am I."
- ☐ Use sticky notes to make predictions as you read a story or novel.
- ☐ Imagine being a character in a story/play – what would you do.
- ☐ Write a letter to the author telling him/her how well you liked (or didn't like) his/her book.

Math

- ☐ Write a series of story problems for others to solve.
- ☐ Learn mathematical operations through songs and jingles, rhythm.
- ☐ Explain how to work a problem to others while they follow.
- ☐ Use a formula card for tests.
- ☐ Make up puns using math vocabulary or terms.
- ☐ Provide tables, graph paper, lines, and space for working problems.
- ☐ Solve problems with a partner: one person solves, and the other explains the process.
- ☐ Make up sounds for different math operations and processes.
- ☐ Create poems telling when to use different math operations.
- ☐ Solve complex story problems in a group.
- ☐ Teach how to use a calculator for problem solving.
- ☐ Do a statistical research project and calculate percentages.
- ☐ Create number sequences and have a partner find the pattern.
- ☐ Use "each one teach one" for new math processes/operations.
- ☐ Mind-map proofs for geometry theorems.
- ☐ Describe everything you do to solve a problem to a partner.
- ☐ Design classification charts for math formulas and operations.
- ☐ Have teams construct problems linking many math operations, then solve them.
- ☐ Do a survey of students' likes/dislikes, then graph the results.
- ☐ Track thinking patterns for different math problems.
- ☐ Estimate measurements by sight and by touch.
- ☐ Bridge math concepts beyond school. (What? So what? Now what?)
- ☐ Add, subtract, multiply, and divide using manipulatives.
- ☐ Imagine using a math process successfully, then really do it.
- ☐ Learn metric measurement through visual equivalents.

Practical Arts & Physical Education

☐ Give verbal explanation of sport routines.

☐ Have students imagine the computer is human – draw how it works.

☐ Have students tell one another how to run a word processing program – then do it.

☐ Have students perform physical exercise routines in sync with music.

☐ Have students pretend they are radio sportscasters describing a game in progress.

☐ Play "Recipe Jeopardy" – make questions for answers given.

☐ Use music to help improve keyboarding skills and speed.

☐ Teach and play a series of non-competitive games.

☐ Use peer-coaching teams for individual shop projects.

☐ Assign teams to prepare and serve meals from foreign countries.

☐ Have students draw pictures of how to perform certain physical feats.

☐ Have students work in pairs to learn and improve sports skills.

☐ Teach a series of "spatial games" (e.g. horseshoes, ring toss).

☐ Create cooperative computing teams to learn computer skills.

☐ Create visual diagrams of how to use shop machines.

☐ Have students list how things learned in shop can help in your future life.

☐ Teach students to imagine a skill, and then try to do it exactly as they imagined.

☐ Capture a process involved in art or sports on video or camera, and create a step-by-step manual or review materials using the images.

☐ Choose textbooks with CD-Rom companion materials.

Science & Health

- ☐ Write a humorous story using science vocabulary.
- ☐ Group research projects in which each group designs and implements plans.
- ☐ Create a diary on "The Life of a Red Blood Cell."
- ☐ Use lab teams for science experiments and exercises.
- ☐ Write steps used in an experiment so someone else can do it.
- ☐ Discuss controversial health topics and write team position papers.
- ☐ Make up an imaginary conversation between parts of the body.
- ☐ Describe the "before and after" of key scientific paradigm shifts.
- ☐ Give a speech on "Ten steps to healthful living."
- ☐ Learn the pattern of successful and reliable scientific experiments.
- ☐ Use the symbols of the Periodic Table of Elements in a story.
- ☐ Practice webbing attributes of various systems of the body.
- ☐ Find five different ways to classify a collection of leaves.
- ☐ Draw pictures of things seen under a microscope.
- ☐ Create montages/collages on science topics (e.g., mammals).
- ☐ Create posters/flyers showing health processes.
- ☐ Use vocabulary games to study and review science vocabulary.
- ☐ Use concrete models to demonstrate science concepts and/or parts.
- ☐ Use concrete models as metaphors for systems in the human body.
- ☐ Use forensic science activities to create interest in scientific method, research, etc.

Chapter 7 Review & Discussion Questions

1. After reviewing this chapter, what adaptations, accommodations, or ideas are most likely to be of benefit to your students today?
2. What adaptation, accommodation, or idea might you adapt for use in your classroom to increase learning, reach more learning styles, and enhance your teaching without reducing rigor?
3. What interventions or adaptations did you find to be the most potentially useful for students with ADD, ADHD, or auditory processing difficulties?

Tools & Activities

After reading the sections of this chapter on:
- Note Taking Strategies
- Reading Comprehension Strategy
- Teaching Vocabulary with Visuals
- Writing Strategies
- Tools & Techniques to Help Students Focus
- Ideas for Differentiating Instruction by Subject

1. Which strategies might you incorporate into your day-to-day teaching to best enhance the learning environment in your classroom?
2. How would you employ these strategies? Provide examples from your current lessons.
3. Which three tools or strategies will enhance critical thinking skills?

Participation Strategies

1. How well do the participation strategies in the chapter promote inquiry, self-monitoring, and self-evaluation?
2. Which teaching techniques that have already been addressed support participation beyond answering a direct question?

Practical Application

Design an activity using a strategy in this book. How will you ensure that all levels of learners are challenged yet not frustrated while completing the activity? What scaffolding will you put in place to increase likelihood of success?

Using the ideas, tools, and techniques in this chapter for reference, adapt or develop your own tool to promote success in your classroom or subject area. If completing this course individually, journal the results of this application with an example of the tool you develop.

✄ **CHAPTER 8** ❧

Strategies that Enhance Recall and Comprehension

Additional Resources

Video Bonus

Navigate to
EduVideo.SusanFitzell.com

To see video explanations
of the strategies
highlighted in this book.

VIDEO
Resources

This book, and the principles discussed within it, are about scientifically supported, classroom tested, best practice teaching. No matter what theories, programs, or vernacular we are currently using in education, some information must be remembered for later recall. This is a simple fact; both of life and of learning.

The strategies outlined in this chapter offer a variety of solutions for helping our students store the information we offer them, and successfully recall that information when they need it again. Also, strategies such as metacognitive mind mapping and attaching learning to real life application support higher level thinking including comprehension, analysis, and evaluation.

Most of these strategies include Nonlinguistic Representation components. Academic research has consistently indicated that creating nonlinguistic representations requires students to think about content in new ways. Students will need to create a representation of new information that does not rely on text or verbal language. Representations need to be meaningful and related to the content. Nonlinguistic representation is more than "just drawing pictures." It is drawing images or maps that represent the information being conveyed in a meaningful way.(Marzano, 2010a)

Visual Strategies

Mind Mapping/Graphic Roadmaps/Visual Organizers

I started using mind mapping after reading *I Can See You Naked: A Fearless Guide to Making Great Presentations* by Ron Hoff. My first presentation was drawn out like a colorful board game with a route to follow, arrows, and picture images of what I was going to do. I remember thinking how much easier it was to use than index cards with a text script written on them. It also was much less restricting. I did not feel tied to reading the cards. Rather, I looked at the picture and went from memory. It saved me from the plight of many presenters: that of being tied to a script.

The technique worked so well for me that I started expanding the idea into my teaching efforts. **As I read selections from English texts to my students, I drew the events out on paper in map and graphic format.** I would often interject silly ditties and exclamations of passion into the effort to make what I was reading to them stick out in their memory. Given my students were at the 'cool' age of 'teen' they would often look at me and say, "You are crazy!" My pat answer was always, "Yes, I am, but you'll remember this because of it." Moreover, they did.

Students learn and remember mind maps better if they create them out of their own mental images and patterns. One can define a mind map as follows: A mind map consists of a central word or concept, around which you draw 5 to 10 main ideas that relate to that central word. You then take each of those 'new' words and again draw 5 to 10 main ideas that relate to each of those words. You can find more information on mind maps on Wikipedia: http://en.wikipedia.org/wiki/Mind_map.

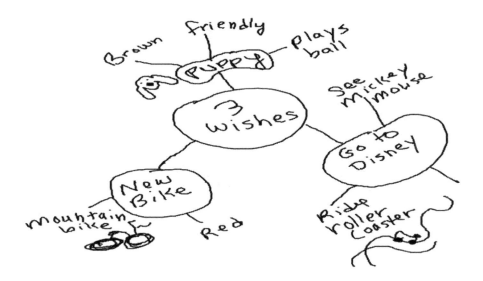

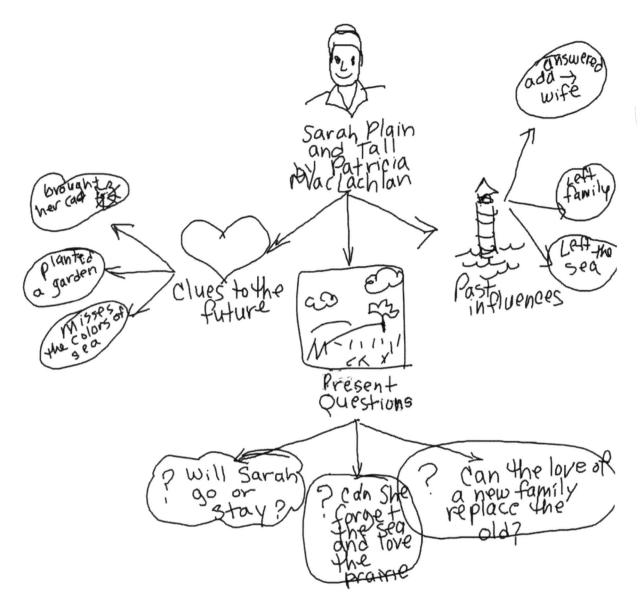

When students make spelling errors at this phase of the creative process, note them, but let them go. Correcting students' spelling while they are creating will cause them to clutter their working memory with rules and not allow enough "space" for coming up with ideas. So correct the difference between 'add' and 'ad' later.

Memory Models

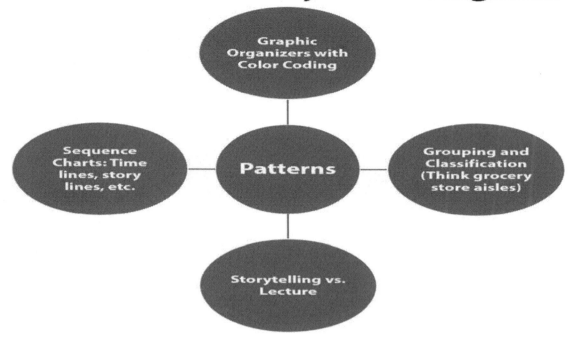

Patterns are the Keys to Intelligence

Ask students to find patterns: Cause and effect, problem and solution, intense drama and down time, for example.

Memory Models for Deeper Understanding and Recall

A memory model provides a three-dimensional model for the memory to work with.[13] I first saw memory models used in a methods workshop on teaching a unit on the ocean. The presenter had physical objects as symbolic representations of ocean processes. It was fascinating.

While teaching a unit on the respiratory system, I use a memory model to introduce the vocabulary for the unit. Again, some students, believing that such things were childish (well, we had to wean them away from such things in upper elementary and middle school to prepare them for being big kids in high school, right?) thought I was crazy. So be it. My attitude is that if it helps them learn, I do not care if they think I am nuts. Memory models are wonderfully useful. They can be time-consuming to prepare the first time, but worth it if your goal is increased retention.

---

[13] Hoff, Ron. *I Can See You Naked: A Fearless Guide to Making Great Presentations.* Kansas City, MO: Andrews and McMeel, 1988.

Respiratory System Mental Model:

		Flap inside = epiglottis Filter = cilia Canister = lung	Mini-maze = Alveoli (demonstrating the exchange of O_2 and CO_2
Diagram used to teach the respiratory system	Corrugated hose = trachea Ribbing in hose = cartilage	Sponge = Lung tissue	Line up "model" in the order they would be in the respiratory system

Mnemonic Devices[14]

Mnemonic. n. A device, such as a formula or rhyme, used as an aid in remembering.

Mnemonics, or the science or art of aiding memory, is an ancient concept. Many people rely on mnemonic devices to help remember what they have learned or need to recall, from grocery lists to people's names to kings and queens or the presidents. What works for one person may not work for another(Mastropieri & Scruggs, 1998).

The following memory devices may help improve retention of information.

Some examples of mnemonics:
- I AM A PERSON: The four Oceans (Indian, Arctic, Atlantic, and Pacific)
- HOMES: Huron, Ontario, Michigan, Erie, and Superior: the Great Lakes in North America

The best are those made up by the student, as they are meaningful to him/her.

Associations

Developing associations is a familiar strategy used to recall information by connecting it to other, more familiar pieces of information. For example,

---

[14] Adapted from the work of Michael DiSpezio, author of *Critical Thinking Puzzles* (Sterling, 1996) for Scientific American Frontiers.

memorizing a sequence of seemingly random digits is easy when that number series is your birth date or street address. Developing associations is also a helpful way to remember new information.

Rhyming

Rhymes and jingles are powerful memory devices (Claussen; Thaut;, 1997). Just think how often you have used the rhyme "Thirty days has September.. ." to recall the number of days within a month.

To use the rhyme technique, all you have to do is make up a rhyme to remember what you want your students to remember. It's fun! If you have students who are musically inclined, encourage them to make up songs to help them remember long pieces of important information, then share them with the rest of the class.

Examples:
- 30 days has September
  April, June, and November

- In 1492, Columbus sailed the ocean blue

- In 1903, the Wright brothers flew free.
  First successful flight

- I before E except after C
  And when saying "A" as in Neighbor or Weigh
  And weird is weird.

Chunking

The brain can only hold three to four pieces of information, or "chunks", in short-term memory at a time. (N Cowan, 2001; Farrington, 2011; Oberauer & Hein, 2012)In order to keep a lot of information in short-term memory, we naturally break it up into more manageable parts by chunking it in a meaningful way.

When reciting a telephone or Social Security number, most people break it up into three chunks. For example, the first and second chunks of a phone number consist of three digits, and the third chunk contains four digits. Here's a series of numbers that, at first glance, appears meaningless:

8005663712

However, once you realize it's a toll-free phone number, chunking the numbers and creating a mnemonic makes the series easier to remember. The mnemonic I created to remember this number – my old '800' number – draws on my background and experience. Someone else trying to remember the same information would come up with a mnemonic that's meaningful to them in order to remember this number.

My mnemonic for this phone number is: *Five watched while big bully 7 blocked 3 from taking his place with friends 1 and 2.*

Chunking is also an excellent strategy for remembering how to spell words.

An example of chunking follows:

Other examples of chunked spelling words:
ALBU QUER QUE
RE NUMER ATION
PENN SYLVAN IA
CZ ECHO SLO VAKIA
LEU KE MIA
RECE IVE
Chunking information and associating it with information we've already learned, whether it's numbers, math formulas, spelling vocabulary, or anything else, helps us remember it more easily.

Acronyms

An acronym is a word formed from the first letter(s) of each word in a phrase or name. For example, **LASER** stands for **L**ight **A**mplification by **S**timulated **E**mission of **R**adiation. Other familiar acronyms are **RADAR**, **REM** sleep, **SCUBA**, **SONAR**, **NASA**, and **ZIP** code. You can make up acronyms to help students remember information. Think of an acronym as a "fun" word or phrase in which each letter stands for the first letter of the item to be recalled.

Acrostics

An acrostic is similar to an acronym, but it takes the first letters of a series of words, lines, or verses to form a memorable phrase. Sometimes the phrase is nonsense, which may help your students remember it! Here are two: Kings Play Cards On Fat Green Stools or King Philip Came Over For Grandma's Soup.

King **i n g d o m** Philip **h y l u m** Came **l a s s** Over **r d e r** For **a m i l y** Grandma's **e n u s** Soup **p e c i e s**

Each word in the acrostic stands for the biological classification hierarchy: Kingdom, Phylum, Class, Order, Family, Genus, and Species. By creating a visual image to go along with the phrase, we're incorporating multiple brain-based principles for memorization. When students make up their own acrostics and draw images to illustrate them, this is an especially powerful tool for memorization.

Strategy to Remember Sequences

Use adding machine tape to create a visual storyline, timeline, or sequence to be memorized.

As your students are reading a textbook or story, have them draw pictures of the important information (characters, historical figures, places, events, etc.) in the order the information is presented on adding machine tape.

For example, say your class is studying Native American practices. When students read about how the Lakota determined directions, they draw a picture representing the concept on the tape. Next the chapter describes what types of information were recorded, such as position of the sun, the moon, neighbor sites, and more. The class draws and labels that information in the same sequence/order that it is described in the textbook. See the following examples:

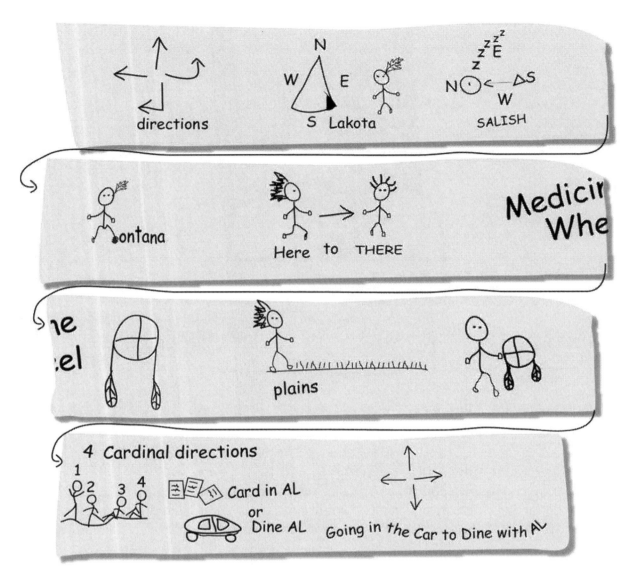

Now your students have a "timeline" or "story line" in sequential order of the practice as described in the textbook or story. This technique can be especially helpful in English and Literature classes; although the novels taught in high school classes rarely come with illustrations, students can draw the storyline in sequential order to remember key characters and the order in which the events in the story take place.

For example, in reading Albert Camus' *The Plague*, students may draw a sequence like the one below. They can make the storyline as detailed as they'd like – or as detailed as they need to remember the key events, triggering the memory when it's time for exams.

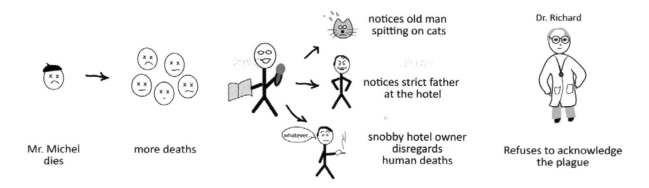

This visual memory tool will help students remember the information in the order that it happened.

Draw It So You'll Know It

Diffusion: Molecules move from an area of high concentration to an area of low concentration

Hive: High concentration of bees (High Hive)
Outside the Hive: Low concentration of bees

Contributed by 7th Grade Science Class, Kennedy Middle School, Waltham MA

Teachers often present information verbally and linguistically. However, many of our students are visual learners. A substantial amount of our brain power is devoted to visual processing. When we add a visual component, a drawing component, to what we are teaching, student recall increases.

225

Consider chunking your lesson plan:
1. Direct teach for 10 minutes.
2. Stop for 3 minutes (set a timer).
3. Instruct students to draw a picture of what you've taught them in the last ten minutes.
4. Have students share their picture with a partner (2 minutes).
5. Ask a few students to share and explain their photos (summarize).
6. Continue with the next chunk of direct teaching or move onto another activity.

When students are reading, or reviewing previously read material...
- Have them draw pictures of what they are reading.
- Have them illustrate their notes with drawings that represent the concepts and facts in their notes.

Although represented in black and white here, this drawing – as well as many of the illustrations throughout this book – was originally created in color.

Color and Memory

Simply put, we remember what we see in color better than what we see in black and white. (Hall & Sidio-Hall, 1994; Wong, 2011)), we remember colors first and content next. Colors affect us on both psychological and physiological levels.

Here are just a few ways you can use color in the classroom:
- Use colored handouts
- Add color to overheads
- Print notes and alternate two colors for each individual point
- Hang colorful posters to reinforce concepts being taught
- Provide colorful visuals

According to the research, color communicates more effectively than black and white. How much more effectively? Here's what the research says:
- Color visuals increase willingness to read by up to 80 percent.[15]
- Using color can increase motivation and participation by up to 80 percent.[11]
- Color enhances learning and improves retention by more than 75 percent.[16]
- Color accounts for 60 percent of the acceptance or rejection of an object and is a critical factor in the success of any visual experience.[17]

The Meaning of Color

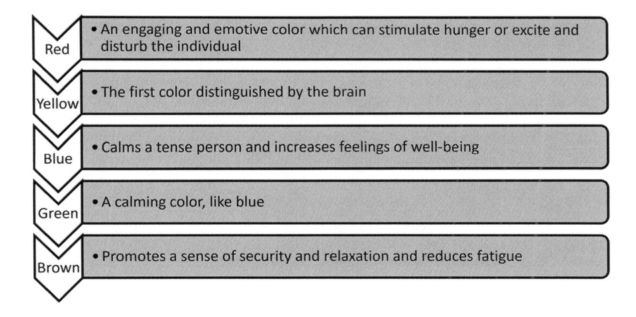

Red
- An engaging and emotive color which can stimulate hunger or excite and disturb the individual

Yellow
- The first color distinguished by the brain

Blue
- Calms a tense person and increases feelings of well-being

Green
- A calming color, like blue

Brown
- Promotes a sense of security and relaxation and reduces fatigue

---

[15]Green, Ronald E. "The Persuasive Properties of Color." *Marketing Communications*, October 1984.
[16] Loyola University School of Business, Chicago, IL., as reported in Hewlett-Packard's *Advisor*, June 1999.
[17] Walker, Morton. *The Power of Color*. New York: Avery Publishing Group, 1991.

Snapshot Devices

Snapshot devices (Siple, Caccamise, & Brewer, 1982) take learning to another level because their purpose is to take a 'snapshot' of what we've just taught and represent it visually so students will remember it.

For instance, let's say you've just taught about the importance of new inventions in settling the Western frontiers, including the six-shooter, the windmill, the sod house, the locomotive, and barbed wire.

A snapshot device is a picture with all the things you've just taught in it. However, rather than a collection of individual pictures, this is a scene – the images are connected, and students will think about the connections. Students will remember the cowboy with the six-shooters and the train coming down the hill behind the sod house. They will see the scene in their minds' eye. You can also assign snapshot devices as homework; having students figure out how to connect related images in this way is much more meaningful than filling out a worksheet!

Three Card Match: Review

Materials
    Index cards
    • Choose three of the following card colors: pink, green, blue, yellow, or white.
    • If you only have white cards or white paper, color-code the cards. For example:
        • Put a yellow dot or stripe on the word cards.
        • Put a green dot or stripe on the picture cards.
        • Put a pink dot or stripe on the definition cards...and so on and so forth.
    Pictures
    • Of the item being reviewed
    • Or related to the concept being reviewed
    • Or mnemonic pictures to form an association

Instructions

1. Break down what students have to memorize into three related concepts, facts, pictures, meanings, etc.
2. Each card should contain one 'item.' (See example below.)
3. Label the back of each card in a set with a number, so children can turn the card over and self-correct.

For example:

- The word elephant, the picture of the elephant and the definition of the elephant would all be numbered #1 on the back.
- The word zebra, the picture of the zebra and the definition of the zebra would all be numbered #2, etc.

el·e·**ph**ant

An enormous mammal with a very long nose called a trunk.

Options for use:

- Students can match the cards on their own as a review in the resource room or classroom. If they have their own sets, they may use them at home to study.
- Students can pair up to match the cards. This is an excellent peer tutoring activity.

Visual Or Mnemonic	Word	Definition
	Folium of Descartes	$x^3 + y^3 == 3x*y$

BEETLES	coleoptera	Wings meet in a straight line, bottom wings are membranous, top wings form a hard cover.
BUTTERFLIES AND MOTHS	lepidoptera	Wings are membranous and covered with scales.
GRASSHOPPERS, CRICKETS & ROACHES	orthoptera	Wings are thin and veined. One pair of legs is more muscular.

The Fitzpell Method of Studying Spelling Words

Option 1: Use phonics rules to determine which letters should be in a **stand-out color**.

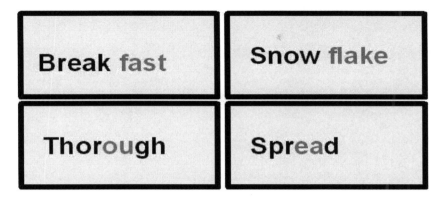

Option 2: Pre-test
Use pre-test errors to determine which letters should be in a **stand-out color**.
Theory: Make the corrected mistake in spelling stand out so the mistake is not repeated.

1. Whenever possible, add clip art pictures to 'visualize' the word.
2. Use bright color markers with good contrast to differentiate.
3. Add any other symbols, sound cues, etc. to make the spelling word more memorable.
4. PRINT the words on INDEX CARDS.
5. Practice by running through the cards two to three times each day for the four days before the spelling test. Put aside the cards that need more study. Cards that can be spelled quickly can be pulled out of the daily second and third run.

Option 3: Put the key words in the question and the key words in the answer in a different color than the rest of the text.

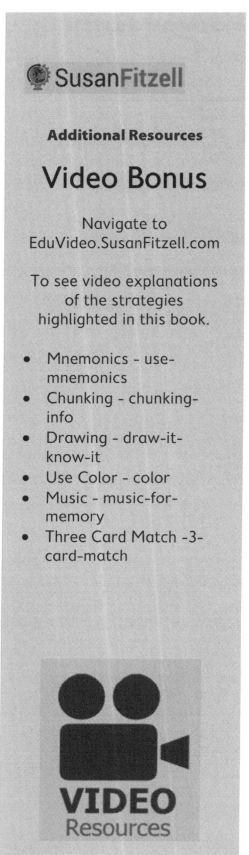

Good luck!
You should see a significant improvement in spelling test grades.

Auditory Strategies

Music as a Memory Strategy

Do you remember the lyrics to songs you listened to when you were a teenager? Can you still remember the words to songs you learned when you were in elementary school? Maybe these songs helped you to learn content such as grammar (Grammar Rock) or math (Multiplication Rock). Songs, chants, and raps help students memorize information and provide a hook for retrieving that information easily later. (Claussen; Thaut;, 1997; Gfeller, 1983; Wallace, 1994)

You and your students can create and perform songs for learning by substituting the lyrics in karaoke songs with the information that must be memorized. Take a nursery rhyme or folk song and substitute the words with the facts students must learn. Whether you purchase ready-made music for learning or create your own, this memorization technique helps students retain what they have learned and provides them with a way to access that information in long-term memory.

Zip Around: Review

Zip Around is an easy and fun way to help students identify patterns, make associations, and provide the repetition necessary to move information to long-term memory. Here's how it works:

1. Pass out index cards with a term or idea on one side and the definition or explanation of a new word on the other side.
2. The teacher, or a student volunteer, starts by reading the definition or explanation on one of the cards.
3. The student with that term or idea on their card stands and says the word, then turns the card over and reads the definition or explanation on their card.
4. The game moves around the room, with the student who has each term or idea standing up and announcing their word, then reading a new definition.
5. The last definition or explanation will match the word on the back of the first definition's card.

After your students get the hang of the game, time them and see how fast they can do it. Associating definitions or explanations to terms or ideas is a novel way to process information and the brain focuses on that novelty. Timing the activity provides another level of uniqueness to the learning. This is drill and practice in a fast and fun way that can help increase recall speed.

Kinesthetic Strategies

Using Movement as a Memory Strategy

Just like any of us, our students get bored with sitting in their seats for hours at a time. We can use this to our benefit – incorporating movement can be powerful for enhancing retention and learning. Movement provides greater levels of oxygen to the brain and involves multiple areas of the brain in the memory process.

Ways to incorporate movement into lessons include:
- Have students act out vocabulary words.
- Create gestures that represent key people, places, or facts from the lesson.
- Teach sign language for learning vocabulary and spelling words.
- Using sports for memorization:
- If you can get access to your school's gym or an outdoor basketball hoop – or even a "kiddie" hoop with Nerf balls in your own classroom – make a game out of stating a fact and then shooting a basket. The rules can be whatever you decide to be most appropriate and get all students involved. The important thing is the movement, fun, and challenge in the activity. If students are divided up into teams, they can help one another, enhancing the learning activity by having students teach each other – without even realizing it!
- If soccer or another sport is easier (for example, if you can't get access to a basketball hoop, but you can get access to a grassy field), you can use that sport as the foundation of the exercise. As long as memorizing information is a part of the rules of the game, you can use whatever rules you'd like.

Here's an example from my own experience: I had an adult martial arts student who was having trouble remembering the Kung Fu forms from one lesson to the next. As an experiment, I had him warm up for a half hour before the lesson. After he started walking the treadmill before each lesson, he started remembering the forms better and advancing much more quickly.

An oxygenated brain "remembers" better.

Make it Meaningful

Bring Emotion into the Lesson

We remember things that evoke our emotion. Advertisers use this knowledge effectively. When we can bring drama into the classroom, we will see increased learning. I will never forget the Western Civilization professor that I had in college and the excitement and passion she demonstrated for her subject. I hated history all through high school. Suddenly, I found myself enjoying a history class. Between my use of mnemonics and the teacher's drama, enthusiasm, and ability to relate what she taught to the real world (including our future), I learned and loved it! Thanks Ms. Civitello!

- Make it a story
- Read with dramatization
- Use a gripping picture

Whenever possible, introduce concepts with pictures that evoke emotions. Many times, we focus on the printed word in texts and make minimal use of the photos. Artwork and drama reach the heart. Use it whenever possible to hook your students into the lesson.

Note: Use Photos as Tools for Brain-Based Learning and Multiple Intelligences.

Attach it to Real Life: Instruction Guide with Students as Stars[18]

"Students are more invested in what they are learning if they can apply it to their lives," explains George Jackman, a high school industrial arts teacher. "Basically, I video the daily happenings, go to the computer desktop publishing station, pick those shots that <u>best</u> demonstrate concepts and words, then build a page."

"To ensure that the students have extended practice opportunities with this information, I create a crossword (with built-in prompts and cues!) that they do for homework. Through this process, students become familiar with practices and concepts. Because the pictures are current (and images of themselves), kids see the exercise as 'real' and of 'quality'; something worth doing." George states with conviction, "I know this is very empowering!"

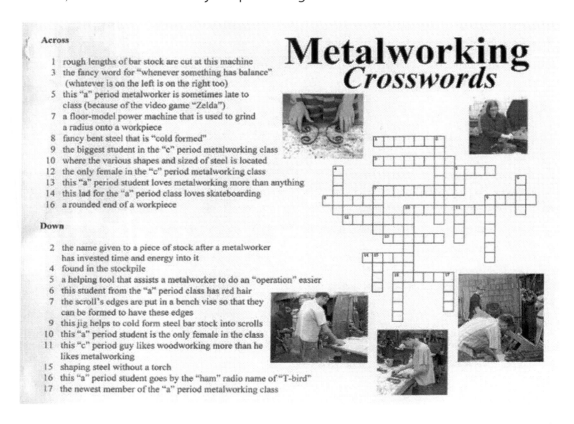

Metalworking Crosswords

Across

1 rough lengths of bar stock are cut at this machine
3 the fancy word for "whenever something has balance" (whatever is on the left is on the right too)
5 this "a" period metalworker is sometimes late to class (because of the video game "Zelda")
7 a floor-model power machine that is used to grind a radius onto a workpiece
8 fancy bent steel that is "cold formed"
9 the biggest student in the "c" period metalworking class
10 where the various shapes and sized of steel is located
12 the only female in the "c" period metalworking class
13 this "a" period student loves metalworking more than anything
14 this lad for the "a" period class loves skateboarding
16 a rounded end of a workpiece

Down

2 the name given to a piece of stock after a metalworker has invested time and energy into it
4 found in the stockpile
5 a helping tool that assists a metalworker to do an "operation" easier
6 this student from the "a" period class has red hair
7 the scroll's edges are put in a bench vise so that they can be formed to have these edges
9 this jig helps to cold form steel bar stock into scrolls
10 this "a" period student is the only female in the class
11 this "c" period guy likes woodworking more than he likes metalworking
15 shaping steel without a torch
16 this "a" period student goes by the "ham" radio name of "T-bird"
17 the newest member of the "a" period metalworking class

---

[18] Contributed by George Jackman, Londonderry High School, Londonderry, NH.

Metalworking Scenes

getting bar stock from the stockpile

cutting to length using the horizontal bandsaw

grinding a radius on both ends using the finishing machine

using a bending jig to "cold form" a scroll shape

the bench vise helps to make a scroll's edges "flush"

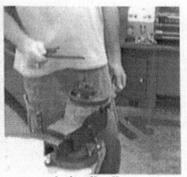

the bending jig

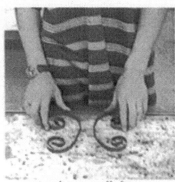

comparing a scroll shape to its matching "workpiece"

comparing a scroll shape for "symmetry"

comparing a scroll shape to check progress

Who Am I? Introduction or Review

Materials
- Index cards or card stock (this can be run through most printers or copiers)
- Nametag pouches with the elastic cords to wear like a necklace
- Source of pictures or a FEW words in print

Instructions
1. Make or buy cards that have a picture or name of a person, place, animal, or thing from the unit you are studying on one side of the card.
2. Make them no wider than a nametag and no taller than four inches.
3. Use cardstock and/or laminate the pieces for longevity and functionality. (They do not work well if the paper is so limp it flops over in the pouch.)
4. Warn each student about the consequences of snapping the elastic cords around another student's neck. Even if you remember to do this, you might have one lively child decide to snap one of the pouches.
5. Students put the pouches around their necks.
6. THEN, so they cannot see you, put or have students put a card representing their identity in the pouch, so that everyone else can see it.
7. The student's goal is to guess his/her identity by going around the room, asking questions to investigate who he/she is.
8. The student may ask ONLY YES or NO questions. Those answering questions must answer only YES or NO.
9. The game is over when all students have guessed their identity, or you call time.

POSSIBLE TOPICS
- _____
- _____
- _____
- _____

Name Tag Pouch available at any office supply store to hold "player identity".

The Leaning Tower of Pisa

This activity makes learning meaningful by attaching new information to previous knowledge.

Chapter 8 Review & Discussion Questions

This chapter covers a variety of teaching strategies and activities that reach multiple learning styles and enhance retention and recall of information.

1. Which strategies might you incorporate into your day-to-day teaching to best enhance the learning environment in your classroom and increase retention in your students?
2. How would you employ these strategies? Provide examples from your current lessons.

Practical Application

Incorporate three of the strategies offered in this chapter into your lesson plans and use them with your classes. Document the results of using each strategy as part of your lessons.

⚕ **CHAPTER 9** ⚕

Assessment & Grading Accommodations

For some, the subject of grading is full of emotion. Some districts have very liberal grading policies, while others are very tightly controlled. Whether you have strong opinions or are simply trying to understand how to accommodate those you must, this chapter offers insights and suggestions for you to, at least, consider.

General Considerations

Grading students with special needs in the regular classroom, especially at the high school level, is a problematic issue. The many opinions, points of view, and philosophies on the subject are often strongly held and emotionally laden. This is a tough one. The key is to find a method of grading in the inclusive classroom that is comfortable for you, the teacher, and fair for _all_ the students.

Standardized tests, most ready-made textbook tests, and many teacher-made pencil and paper tests seldom provide a fair assessment of the special needs learner. In all my years of teaching experience, I have rarely seen students with special needs test well. I have often seen students do well on all coursework except tests. I have also seen students go down an entire letter grade because of a final exam.

If students can demonstrate understanding and knowledge in every other aspect of the class except tests, what do the tests prove? Standardized and traditional pencil and paper tests are a better indicator of short-term memory capability than acquisition of knowledge, comprehension of material, and application of knowledge.

Options to Traditional Grading Systems

- Contract grading often provides clear expectations and achievable chunks for students. The student knows what is needed to acquire a grade and can work toward that goal. Often, students are clueless as to how their individual pieces of work figure into the final "grade." A contract provides a clear structure for students to work within.
- Provide a structure where effort, behavior, preparedness, and prompt attendance are rewarded. These traits are important in the workplace and should be reinforced in school. I give students five points per day based on these factors. It averages out to 20% of their grades. I would tell my students that if they did all their class work and homework to the best of their ability (50% of their grade); they could not fail my class even if they were horrible test takers (30%). This system worked for most of my students. They all knew they could earn a minimum of a *C* no matter how badly they did on tests. See Class Points Chart in Chapter 4: Tools & Activities.
- Use a variety of assessment tools so that all learning styles are accommodated. The assessment tools used have a major impact on the grade earned. Even at the college level, a variety of assessment tools and methods are often used. The argument that pencil and paper testing prepares students for college is not accurate.

What Constitutes a Lowered Grade?[19]

Here is a reasonable guideline to follow based on current research and litigation.

If a student is receiving adaptations:
- He or she should be evaluated and graded similar to that of the general student population.
- The adaptations do not need to be indicated on the report card.

Adaptations are a civil rights issue.

If a student is receiving significant curriculum modifications
(curriculum content is reduced >33%), then:
- Pass/fail or credit/no-credit might be used on the report card.
- The school may change the course number for that student to indicate a different curriculum while in the general classroom *if that course option is available to the general population*. It is imperative that any report card designations do not discriminate.
- Teachers *must* explain modified grades to parents.
- You may put info on reports that go home, but not on the permanent record.

Examples:
- Give a student a calculator = NO impact on grades
- Oral vs. written = NO impact on grades
- Reducing the number of problems = NO impact on grades
- Consistently and significantly reducing the number of vocabulary words learned in English = May impact grades
- If the student is meeting two-thirds of the curriculum, let it go.

Grading systems for all students must have a rationale that addresses both standards and special needs and be implemented throughout a school.

Research indicates that grading policies and practices, including adaptations, should be clearly explained to all students before they are made, with a compelling rationale provided. Because both teachers and students seem to feel that effort should be recognized in some way, this may be a good place to start for reaching some consensus about grading adaptations.

---

[19] Adapted from *Successful Co-Teaching Strategies* by Dr. Marilyn Friend, <www.marilynfriend.com>.

What is Fair?

In studies done by Munk, Bursuck, and Olson, (Bursuck, Munk, & Olson, 1999; Munk & Bursuck, 1998) the following observations were made:

Teachers may change grading criteria by
- Varying grading weights (e.g., varying how much certain criteria count toward a grade).
- Modifying curricular expectations (e.g., identifying an individualized curriculum on which to base a grade).
- Using contracts and modified course syllabi (e.g., teacher and student agreeing on quality, quantity, and timelines for specific work).
- Grading based on improvement (e.g., assigning extra points for improvement over previous performance).

Same subject,
Same curriculum,
Same level: Different teacher

Will all students be graded the same? Equally?

What's fair?

In addition to changes made to the criteria for grading, teachers may adapt the actual letter and number grades by
- Adding written comments (e.g., adding comments to clarify the criteria used to determine a letter grade).
- Adding information from a student activity log (e.g., keeping written anecdotal notes indicating student performance in specific areas over time).
- Adding information from portfolios or performance-based assessments (e.g., collecting student work that measures effort and progress).
- Under some circumstances, teachers may elect to implement alternatives to letter and number grades. Such adaptations include pass-fail grades and competency checklists.

Teachers felt the following adaptations were most helpful to students with disabilities:
- Pass-fail grades
- Checklists
- Written comments

Teachers indicated that letter and number grades could be adapted for students with disabilities (in descending order of perceived helpfulness) by
- Basing grade on process versus product.

- Basing grade on amount of improvement.
- Basing grade on progress on IEP objectives.
- Adjusting grading weights based on assignment and ability.
- Basing grade on criteria defined in an individual contract.

Teachers indicated that letter and number/percentage grades are more useful for students without disabilities, whereas pass/fail grades are more useful for students with disabilities.

Regarding fairness, 73% of the teachers felt that making report card adaptations *only* for students with disabilities was unfair. Most teachers, however, said that the reason the adaptations would be unfair was that adaptations were made available only to students with disabilities, not necessarily because they represented a lowering of standards or a lack of consistency.

In fact, 50% of the teachers reported using specific adaptations for students without disabilities. **This finding suggests that teachers may be quite flexible when they think adaptations will benefit [all] their students.**

Consider This:
If a teacher *adapts* by using knowledge and guiding principles of learning style, multiple intelligences, and brain-based research, couldn't that teacher consistently *adapt* for all students as their needs indicate? Would that not be fair?

Assessment Accommodations

What Is an Assessment Accommodation?

- An assessment accommodation is an alteration in the way a test is administered or the way a student takes a test.
- Assessment accommodations are designed to respond to a student need. Assessment accommodations generally refer to changes that do not alter what the test measures.
- They are not intended to give the student an unfair advantage.
- Students with disabilities may use assessment accommodations to show what they know without being impeded by their disabilities.
- IEPs must include a statement of any individual modifications in the administration of state or district-wide assessments of student achievement that are needed in order for the child to participate in the assessment.
- In general, no accommodation should ever be recommended for a student unless that student also has an opportunity to use it during instructional activities.

Guiding Principles

- Do not assume that every student with disabilities needs assessment accommodations.
- The IEP team must determine the accommodations.
- Base accommodations on student need.
- Be respectful of the student's cultural and ethnic background.
- Integrate assessment accommodations into classroom instruction.
- Know whether your state and/or district has an approved list of accommodations.
- Plan early for accommodations.
- Include students in decision making.
- Understand the purpose of the accommodation.
- Request only those accommodations that are truly needed.
- Determine if the selected accommodation requires another accommodation.
- Provide practice opportunities for the student.
- Remember that accommodations in test taking won't necessarily eliminate frustration for the student.

Types of Accommodations

Timing Accommodations
- Frequent breaks
- Extended time

Scheduling Accommodations
- Over several days
- Order of subtests
- Specific time of day

Setting Accommodations
- Preferential seating
- Separate location
- Specialized setting

Presentation Accommodations
- Different editions
- Read test/directions
- Prompts
- Clarification
- Templates
- Markers
- Secure paper to desk
- Magnifying/amplification devices
- Reread directions

Response Accommodations
- Student marks booklet
- Verbal response
- Special paper
- Math tools
- Reference materials
- Technology
- Point to answer

Specific Test Adaptations

- Administer tests orally in a one-on-one setting.
- Add a word bank.
- Highlight multiple-choice items.
- Peer "test" using a game such as Three Card Match.
- Break the test into smaller chunks.
- Add white space.
- Make sure wording and directions are clear and concrete.
- Read the test orally to a small group.
- Assign a project that demonstrates learning.
- Create crossword-format tests and quizzes.
- Provide pictures as cues.
- Weighed grading of tests: Only grade what the student is accountable for and/or for concepts tested rather than quantity of test items.
- Use portfolio assessment.
- Use performance assessments.
- Allow the use of a spell checker, word processor, or speech-to-text for essay questions.
- Give individual help with directions during tests.
- Simplify wording of test questions.
- Give practice questions as a study guide.
- Give extra help preparing for tests.
- Provide extended time to finish tests.
- Use black and white copies.
- Give feedback to individual student during test.
- Highlight key words in questions.
- Give frequent quizzes rather than relying on exams.
- Allow students to answer fewer questions while still covering all content.
- Allow oral instead of written answers (e.g., tape recorders).
- Give the actual test as a study guide.
- Change the question type (e.g., essay to multiple choice or multiple choice to essay) with the opportunity to answer orally.
- Teach students test taking skills.
- Use tests with enlarged print.
- Test on lesser content than rest of the class.
- Provide extra space on tests for answering.
- Give open-book/notes tests.
- Allow answers in outline format.
- Give take-home tests.

Educate students about the purpose of accommodations. Assure them that the accommodations aren't just for "stupid" kids. If they need privacy to use an accommodation, try to change the setting so that perceived stigma is reduced.

Consider if teachers make accommodations on a regular basis in their classrooms based on students' learning styles and multiple intelligences, then there will be much less stigma attached to the student who chooses to use a needed accommodation.

Student input is critical in selecting accommodations. If a student does not like an accommodation, he or she will not use it. Two key questions to ask a student about a proposed accommodation are:
- "Does this help you?"
- "Will you use this accommodation?"

Most states have an approved list of accommodations.
These can vary widely from one state to the next.

Note. Adapted from *Classroom Grading: A National Survey of Policies* (Polloway et al., 1994)

Grading Options Quick List

- Give a separate grade for process and for product/content.
- A math test has one grade for "demonstrated work" and another grade for final answers.
- An English paper has one grade based on the steps the student completed to fulfill the rubric or paper's requirements and another grade for the final product.
- A science lab may have one grade to reflect the attention to detail, effort, patience and neatness of the lab and another grade for the final product.
- *Teachers typically grade only the final product. Grading for both motivates and gives credit to students for their efforts on the assignment or test.
- Grade on improvement shown.
- Grade on effort shown.
- Traditional letter grading system.
- Pass/Fail options.
- Differentiated syllabi – Contract for grades based on syllabi chosen. Content same – process different.
- Weighted grades within the class setting; for example, major tests count least, class work counts most.
- Co-teachers share grading.
- Portfolio summaries.
- Grade based on rubrics.
- Grades adjusted to student ability.
- Grades are based on less content than the rest of the class.
- Grade based on IEP goals.
- Give audio feedback on drafts of tests and projects before final grading.
- Use the MEDIAN instead of the MEAN for grading.

Which grade truly reflects the student's overall knowledge?

78	98	100
78	93	93
75	88	80
75	86	80
73	62	80
72	0	79
69		75
68	Median 87	63
45	Mean: 71	60
0		0
		0
Median: 72.5		Median: 79
Mean: 63		Mean: 65

An Alternative to the Traditional Quiz

The best alternative to testing is demonstration of knowledge. Whenever possible, have students do a project, write a paper, do an analysis, and/or apply knowledge learned. Here's a fun and effective way to quiz students.

Three Card Match: Peer Tutor or Peer Quiz

Materials:
- Matching cards from Three Card Match game (see examples in the previous chapter)
- Quarter (coin)

Instructions:

1. Pair up students. (Matching ability is not necessary and may be less successful.)
2. Allow students to peer practice by matching the cards before the "quiz."
3. Students MUST ensure each one of their pair knows how to match all the cards.
4. Instruct students that once a pair of students is confident that they can match the cards each on their own, they should notify you that they are ready for the quiz.
5. Have the pair call heads or tails.
6. Flip a coin.
7. The person who calls tails takes the quiz.
8. That student has to match the cards by himself/herself on-the-spot for you to see.
9. Both students get the same quiz grade.

Assessment? Well, I Quiz Every Friday...

How we assess students to determine their understanding of the content that we are teaching is critical to the Response to Intervention process. Schools are becoming more and more locked into using:

- Summative assessment
- Standardized measures of student achievement
- Multiple-choice tests
- And other traditional forms of written assessment

> *Although one could make an argument that this must be the measure that teachers use because it is the measure required for state testing, it is truly an inaccurate, and I would argue unethical, means of evaluating students.*

The only true evaluation is authentic assessment. Authentic assessments incorporate a variety of measures into the evaluation process and focuses on formative assessment. Some types of authentic assessment include:

- Rubrics
- Exit cards
- Curriculum-based measurement
- Student self-evaluation
- Documented observations

> *When assessing with a variety of measures, teachers build a portfolio of data that provides a more accurate picture of the student as a learner. With this authentic, data-driven student portrait, teachers have the necessary information to do the problem solving and detective work required for determining appropriate interventions.*

For example, when students are engaged in drawing what they've learned (a nonlinguistic learning strategy), the teacher can circumnavigate the room holding an observation record sheet and assess a student's understanding by looking at their drawings and asking questions for clarification. Document the observations, and we have a form of authentic and immediate ongoing assessment.

Progress Monitoring versus What We Have Done Historically

Traditional Assessments

- Typically, lengthy and time consuming

- Administered infrequently or at the end of a unit

- Typically students do not receive immediate feedback

Progress Monitoring

- Easy and quick method for gathering student performance data

- Administered frequently

- Students & teachers receive immediate feedback to adjust instruction

- Excerpted from *RTI Strategies for Secondary Teachers* by Susan Gingras Fitzell (S. G. Fitzell, 2011)

Curriculum-Based Measurement (CBM)

Curriculum-Based Measurement is one form of scientifically based method for Progress Monitoring.

Curriculum-Based Measurements:
- Describe academic competence
- Track academic development
- Improve student achievement
- Three Purposes of Curriculum-Based Measurement:
- Screening
- Progress monitoring
- Instructional diagnosis

Additional quick assessments might include:
- High Fluency Phrases which can be found in *The Fluent Reader*, by Timothy V. Rasinski. I found them with an Internet search on a paper titled, "Phrases and Short Sentences for Repeated Reading Practice."
- Every Day Edits are also effective as both an assessment and an intervention. Search for Every Day Edits at www.educationalworld.com.

Exit Cards

The use of exit cards is a simple assessment tool. Each card will have a set of just two or three questions for students to answer after you teach a lesson. Students answer the questions before the bell rings. It's the last thing they do in class. They must hand it to the teacher before they walk out the door, hence the name "exit cards." It's ongoing, immediate assessment in action.

 If you have two teachers, you have two people who can assess and group the exit cards. Exit cards (a.k.a. "tickets to leave") are used to gather information on student readiness levels, understanding of concepts just taught, interests, and/or learning profiles.

Use the exit ticket data to group students for peer assisted learning or same ability groups.

Exit Card Flexible Grouping Combinations

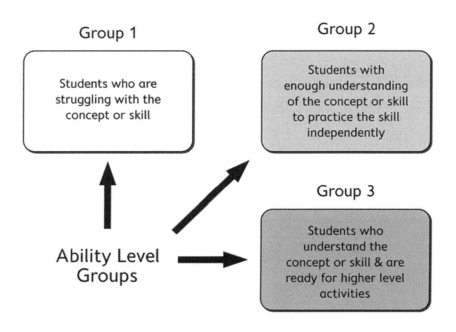

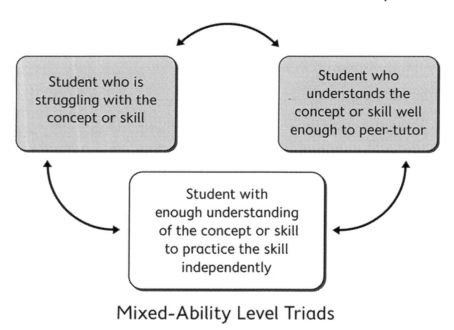

EXIT CARD GROUPINGS - Small Groups

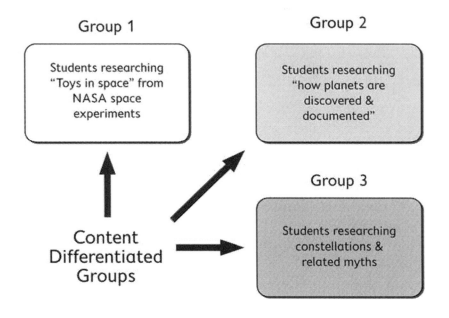

EXIT CARD GROUPINGS - Small Groups

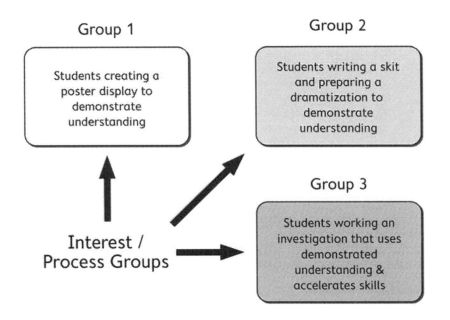

Peer Partners: High/Middle & Middle/Low Technique

Often, teachers will pair a student who is being more successful with a student who is struggling. Consequently, the highest students may be frequently paired with the student with the lowest grades. That can create issues for both the students and some parents.

Another option is to sort your gradebook by grade rather than alphabet (just for this purpose). Then, divide the list in half as shown in the diagram.

Chose a student from the top and pair that student with a student just below the middle. Then, repeat the process so that all students are paired.

It's also a great way to form mixed ability groups of four. Divide the list into quadrants and then choose a student from each quadrant to create a mixed ability group of four.

Because the grades will change over time, the groups will also change. This benefits students on all levels.

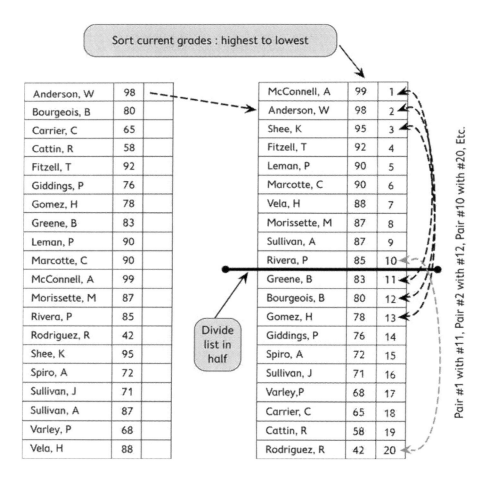

Grade Review Sheet

When students track their progress, achievement goes up! Have you ever handed a report card or progress report to a student and were met with a look of shock? "I got a D? I didn't know my grade was that low!" After teaching for a few years, we hear that all too often.

But there's also a body of knowledge that supports the practice. Robert J Marzano references fourteen different studies where teachers had students in one class track their progress while students in another class did not. Students who tracked their progress typically had a 32-percentile point gain in their achievement over students who did not track their progress. (Marzano, 2010b)

Have students collect data on the Grade Review Sheet and then graph the results!

Team Name:	Grade Review Sheet	Quarter:	
Name:		Class:	

ASSIGNMENT	HW	CW	QUIZZES	TESTS
TITLE, DATE, GRADE	%	%	%	%

- **Include DATE, TITLE AND GRADE for each assignment received.**
- **This grade list should be kept in the front of your binder!**

Should Tests be the Final Measure of Student Success?

As teachers, most of us have been taught that tests are the best way to assess our students' learning (and the effectiveness of our teaching). But when a student scores poorly on a test, how does he or she benefit? The student loses confidence and ends up feeling 'stupid.' I believe we can use tests to improve learning, not just check what our students have memorized.

In his conference remarks, Thomas Guskey challenges teachers to consider how we might change the culture of classroom testing. Guskey asks, "What happens to these tests? What educational purpose do they serve?" His point is that teachers typically grade tests, give them back, and then move on. Students put their tests away and never look at them again. Some students will even make a show of sauntering to the trash to crumple and toss their test in the bin. If a student feels like she studied hard for a test and still got a bad grade, she can become disillusioned and disheartened with the classroom cycle that consists of teaching and testing, teaching and testing.

Many times, testing simply feels like a win or lose game between students and their teacher. I'll never forget the day my son and I were discussing testing in one of his least favorite classes (and with his least favorite teacher) and he looked me square in the eyes and said, "Mom, I refuse to play the game." My son was in honors classes, yet he felt this way! What if his tests were used as a learning tool instead of a 'gotcha'? Would it be perceived as less of a game if students had a chance to re-take the test, or work out where they'd gone wrong?

There is an argument for the exam as the final assessment: if students don't have the knowledge by the time they're tested, that's unfortunate, but it's time to move on – there's only so much time to teach the material. "What about a surgeon? Do they 'test' their learning on a genuine patient?" Guskey asks. "Or do they get to check their learning on a cadaver to make sure they've got it worked out?" You wouldn't show a surgeon a heart bypass in a textbook and then send him or her straight into the operating room!

Tests give us crucial insight into areas where students are struggling. By moving on immediately after giving an exam, teachers miss a valuable opportunity to teach students exactly what they need to learn! Rather than a game in which students either win or lose, teachers can turn testing into a win-win classroom experience by giving students the opportunity to learn from their mistakes. We can change the culture in our classrooms by using tests as a tool to facilitate learning rather than marking the end of the learning process.

Here's an example of how this type of learning can be applied. Let's say you are finishing a unit. For the first part of the lesson, students take a typical test that you quickly grade as they're being handed in. From the test, you can identify 'grey areas' where a significant number of students have struggled and 'failed.' You spend the second part of the class period re-teaching these 'grey' elements. Students are then allowed to re-take this part of the test where, of course, they improve. Rather than feeling disillusioned, students feel empowered and motivated to 'learn from their mistakes.'

After hearing Guskey speak, I reflected on my own experiences. When I was in graduate school, the method of learning was an iterative process, where we continually redrafted our work until it was up to standard. There was no formal testing, but the same piece of work would sometimes be returned six or seven times with feedback. I would read the professor's comments and learn how to improve my work – no disillusionment, just improvements. I learned more than I had in any test-driven educational program, and I actually remembered what I'd learned.

The next time you're preparing a test, consider how you might make it into a learning tool. You may be surprised to find that you can turn your tests into a positive learning experience for all of your students.

Chapter 9 Review & Discussion Questions

1. After reviewing the chapter, what changes, adaptations, or adjustments to your current grading system, if any, do you intend to adopt in, or adapt for, your classroom? Why, or why not?
2. Where will you start to adjust your lessons to provide differentiated instruction to accommodate all levels of learners and learning styles in your classroom?
3. What specific grading strategies will you employ in your classroom, moving forward?
4. How will you employ the use of exit cards in your classroom to provide more immediate and timely ongoing assessment?

Practical Application

Brainstorm and design a grading and assessment strategy for your classroom that incorporates the principles outlined in the chapter and your responses to the questions above.

How to Facilitate a Successful Book Study

Individual Book Study

This book is designed to serve as both a functional reference as well as a textbook that can be used as part of a formal course, individual book study, or guided group study.

Completing the book study as an individual is a simple process:
1. Read the chapter.
2. Consider the Chapter Review/Discussion Questions and jot down or record your thoughts.

NOTE: If you intend to obtain a Verification of Completion for this course, or wish to apply for graduate credit using this book study, you may need to provide copies of your responses to these questions.

3. Implement techniques and strategies in your day-to-day classroom teaching process as outlined (Required for graduate credit).

Group Oriented Book Study

We encourage you to complete this book study as part of a community of learners, where possible:

- Department or grade level teams.
- Core academic teams.
- Vertical teams (across grade level), by subject area.
- Any other reasonable grouping technique that works for your campus or activity.

Each group will need a group facilitator or team leader.

1. Determine your groups or teams.
2. Clearly outline a **timeline** of reading goals.
3. Set dates and times to meet for group discussion of Review/Discussion Questions and application of strategy ideas.
4. Establish ground rules. Use the section in the book on setting ground rules for students as an action learning activity for the group. Simply adjust the activity for adult learners.

Tips for Being a Good Facilitator

- Create a relaxed atmosphere for the group.
- Treat everyone with respect.
- Consider having a co-facilitator, especially for larger groups.

Remember that the term "facilitator" means "to make easy." Your job is to make it easy for everyone to participate. This will help participants feel comfortable and foster an atmosphere of helpful cooperation for everyone, including you.

Be prepared – Understand the chapter Review/Discussion questions. The facilitator is responsible for keeping the discussion on target and allowing everyone to have a voice in discussion.

First Meeting

- Be sure all group members have a book.
- Have all group members introduce themselves, if necessary.
- Be sure everyone understands the purpose and goals of the study.
- Review the course requirements, proposed timeline, and meeting schedule.

All Meetings

- Ask group members to bring their books and notes to every meeting.
- A good way to start is to review the Review/Discussion questions and go over the pages of the book that may apply to the questions.
- The goal of group meetings is to be sure that all members have completed the chapter exercises, promote discussion, and foster an environment of mutual motivation and cooperation.

Review/Discussion Questions and this Guide

- This guide, and the questions offered in each chapter, are meant to promote thought. Let discussion flow and progress naturally.
- If conversation wanders from the topic, return to the discussion questions, but remember that good discussion is sometimes more important than covering all the questions.
- Try to involve everyone.

Leading Discussions

- Pose one question, or scenario, at a time to the group.
- Pre-select the questions or scenarios to discuss, based on group and school needs. Write each on an index card and pass them out to the group members. Each participant (or team of two or three) takes a card and addresses the question or scenario on their card.
- Have participants model strategies discussed in the reading to address questions or scenarios (Mind maps, mnemonics, snapshot devices, etc.)

Group Discussions Without a Facilitator

If the group facilitator is unable to attend and no alternate has been designated, continue with the meeting and discussion without them.

- Take turns going around the room, allowing each group member to talk about his or her experience or thoughts on the reading. Set a time limit for discussion of each participant's comments.
- Hand out index cards. Ask everyone to write a question or observation; then select one or more to discuss. Set time limits for discussion of each card.

Book Study Activities

The fishbowl exercise allows the facilitator to demonstrate how a book study works, and what good facilitation looks like.

Ask for a few volunteers (6 to 8 max) and seat them in a circle with an experienced facilitator inside the "fishbowl." (You can facilitate this group, or have another skilled facilitator do it.) The other participants can sit or stand around the small group to observe. The facilitator begins by welcoming everyone, initiating introductions, and explaining the impartial role of the facilitator.

The facilitator will help the group set its ground rules. Then the discussion begins and continues for several minutes. During the discussion, the facilitator should introduce some typical opening session questions such as personal concerns about the issue, and also some questions that help people consider different viewpoints on the issue (typical of later study circle sessions). During the fishbowl, the facilitator should demonstrate some paraphrasing, clarifying, summarizing, or other common facilitation techniques. Involve the entire group in debriefing the exercise, using the questions below.

Post these questions where everyone can see them in the debriefing demonstration after the fishbowl activity.

What did the facilitator do to:
- Set a positive tone?
- Explain and help the group set the ground rules?
- Help people connect their concerns and values to the issue?
- Manage the discussion process? For example, what interventions did he or she use?
- Were those techniques effective? Would another approach have been better?
- Help advance the group's understanding of the content?
- Make sure that a number of different views were considered?
- Bring out some of the complexities of the issue?
- Try to involve everyone in the discussion?
- Help participants identify areas of general agreement?

Search-Pair-Share

Purpose: To increase the amount of information sharing from a search.

Time	Facilitator Activities	Participant Activities	Techniques & Equipment
30 min	Provide information on *<insert topic>* for research	Identify reference material for *<insert topic>*	Pairs, text, flip chart paper, markers.
10 min	Collect and comment on sources and debrief activity	List sources Discuss aids to process	Whole group

Activity Explanation and Instructions:

Facilitator: When an activity to address a specific standard is needed that also meets the needs of all learners, it may be difficult to locate one. It is easier when material has been previewed, and references are organized in advance.

Objective: Identify the topic to be addressed: *<insert topic>* a nd create a list of suggestions from the text to address that issue or topic while meeting the needs of different participants.

Techniques/Equipment: Written text materials, flipcharts and markers, etc. Monitor and encourage participation.

Process: In pairs:
- Find as many activities, ideas, etc. to effectively address *<insert topic>* in the text within the next [10] minutes.
- Summarize the activity/idea and main points.

Group Success: All participants can explain the main points.

Accountability: Pairs share their references and information with the whole group. A combined list of references is created.

Debrief: What were the differences that you saw in how your pair and other pairs searched for references? How did this affect the length of the compiled list?

Pair, Read, Respond

Purpose: To increase comprehension by using shared readings.

Time	Facilitator Activities	Participant Activities	Techniques & Equipment
25 min	Provide section/chapter information on reading & guide activity	Describe information on *<insert topic>*	Pairs, written information
10 min	Ensure comprehension Debrief activity	Answer content questions Discuss group process	Whole group

Activity Explanation and Instructions:

Objective: Describe *<insert content>*

Time: 35 minutes (5 min set up, 2x10 for pair reading, 10 min debrief)

Techniques/Equipment: One copy of *<insert content>* information to each person. Monitor and encourage participation.

Process: Individually – Silently read each paragraph or section and then, in pairs:
- Take turns describing the content of the reading to their partner. Discrepancies in understanding are discussed as needed.
- When each pair finishes, they might discuss the entire passage.

Group Success: Both people in the group can describe the passage content.

Accountability: Randomly answer questions on content.

Debrief: Was this an effective means of covering this material for you? Why or why not?

What Worries You?

Purpose: To bring out fears so that they can be addressed and handled. Change is difficult. So much is at stake for teachers in today's classrooms that, sometimes, putting those fears out "on the table" for discussion is the best way to address them.

Time	Facilitator Activities	Learner Activities	Techniques & Equipment
10 min	Pose *<insert topic area>* and ask for "nightmares" Guide activity	Identify the worst case scenarios that you can imagine for *<insert topic>*	Pairs, 5x7 cards, markers or felt pens
10 min	Collect cards for reference Debrief activity	Discuss scenarios and perceptions	Whole group

Activity Explanation and Instructions:

Facilitator: What we don't know how to deal with may make us quite nervous.

Objective: Identify imaginary but realistic worst case scenarios for *<insert topic>* situations.

Time: 20 minutes

Techniques/Equipment: Large sticky notes or 5x7 cards, colored markers or felt pens.

Process:
- Individually – Each participant writes out a <insert topic> scenario that they dread (real or imagined).
- In pairs – Discuss the worst case for each scenario.

Group Success: Both participants can identify with the feelings of the other.

Accountability: Scenarios are described to the whole group. Group posts scenarios for review.

Debrief: How does discussing "worst case scenarios" change your perception of what might happen and what you might do about it?

273

Bibliography

Alivisatos, A. P., Chun, M., Church, G. M., Greenspan, R. J., Roukes, M. L., & Yuste, R. (2012). The brain activity map project and the challenge of functional connectomics. *Neuron, 74*(6), 970–4. http://doi.org/10.1016/j.neuron.2012.06.006

Arie van Deursen. (2016). Asking Students to Create Exam Questions | Arie van Deursen. Retrieved February 2, 2017, from https://avandeursen.com/2016/07/24/asking-students-to-create-exam-questions/

Aronson, Elliot; Patnoe, S. (1997). *The Jigsaw Classroom: Building Cooperation in the Classroom* (2nd editio). New York: Longman.

Ausubel, D. P. (1963). *The Psychology of Meaningful Verbal Learning: An introduction to school learning.* New York: Grune and Stratton.

Balkom, S. (1992). *Cooperative Learning. Education Research Consumer Guide.* Washington DC.

Barrett, W. (2001). *Rudy!: An Investigative Biography of Rudy Giuliani.* New York: Basic Books.

Barrow, M. A. (2014). Even math requires learning academic language. *Phi Delta Kappan, 95*(6), 35. http://doi.org/10.1177/003172171409500608

Bell, F. (2005). *Total Body Learning: Movement and Academics*. Manchester: Cogent Catalyst Publications.

Bodie, G. D., Vickery, A. J., Cannava, K., & Jones, S. M. (2015). The Role of "Active Listening" in Informal Helping Conversations: Impact on Perceptions of Listener Helpfulness, Sensitivity, and Supportiveness and Discloser Emotional Improvement. *Western Journal of Communication, 79*(2), 151–173. http://doi.org/10.1080/10570314.2014.943429

Brock, M. E., & Carter, E. W. (2013). A systematic review of paraprofessional-delivered educational practices to improve outcomes for students with intellectual and developmental disabilities. *Research and Practice for Persons with Severe Disabilities, 38.* http://doi.org/10.1177/154079691303800401

Burnett, S. (n.d.). The A-Z of Differentiated Instruction.

Bursuck, W. D., Munk, D. D., & Olson, M. M. (1999). The Fairness of Report Card Grading Adaptations. *Journal for Special Educators, 20*(2), 84–105. http://doi.org/10.1177/074193259902000205

Caine, R. N., Caine, G., McClintic, C., Klimek, K. J., & Costa, A. L. (n.d.). *12 brain/mind learning principles in action : teach for the development of higher-order thinking and executive function.*

Chubbs, C. (2017). Standing vs Sitting Time in Stand-Biased Classrooms. *American Journal of Public Health, 107*(3), e4–e4. http://doi.org/10.2105/AJPH.2016.303617

Claussen; Thaut; (1997). Music as a Mnemonic Device for Children with Learning Disabilities. *Canadian Journal of Music Therapy, 5,* 55–66.

Conderman, G., & Hedin, L. R. (2015). Using Cue Cards in Inclusive Middle School Classrooms. *The Clearing House: A Journal of Educational Strategies, Issues and Ideas*, *88*(5), 155–160. http://doi.org/10.1080/00098655.2015.1061971

Cooper, K. J. (1999, November 26). Study Says Natural Classroom Lighting Can Aid Achievement. *The Washington Post*.

Cowan, N. (2001). The magical number 4 in short-term memory: a reconsideration of mental storage capacity. *The Behavioral and Brain Sciences*, *24*(1), 87-114–85.

Cowan, N. (2010). The Magical Mystery Four: How is Working Memory Capacity Limited, and Why? *Current Directions in Psychological Science a Journal of the American Psychological Society*, *19*(1), 51–57. http://doi.org/10.1177/0963721409359277

Daniels, M. (2000). Dancing with Words: Signing for Hearing Children's Literacy. Open Library: Bergin & Garvey.

Davidson, N. (1971). The Small Group-Discovery Method as Applied in Calculus Instruction. *The American Mathematical Monthly*, *78*(7), 789–791.

Demorest, S. M., & Morrison, S. J. (2000). Does Music Make You Smarter? *Music Educators Journal*. http://doi.org/10.2307/3399646

Durie, R. (2006). An Interview With Howard Gardner. *Mindshift Connection*. Saint Paul: Zephyr Press.

Ellis, A. (1999). Rational Emotive Behavior Therapy as an internal control psychology. *Journal of Rational-Emotive & Cognitive-Behavior Therapy*, *18*(1), 19–38.

Farrington, J. (2011). Seven plus or minus two. *Performance Improvement Quarterly*, *23*(4), 113–116. http://doi.org/10.1002/piq.20099

Fitzell, S. (2010). *Paraprofessionals and Teachers Working Together: Highly Effective Strategies for Inclusive Classroom*. Cogent Catalyst Publications.

Fitzell, S. G. (1997). *Free the children!: Conflict Education for Strong Peaceful Minds* (Reprint). Manchester: Cogent Catalyst Publications.

Fitzell, S. G. (2007). *Transforming anger to personal power : an anger management curriculum for grades 6-12*. Champaign: Research Press.

Fitzell, S. G. (2011). *RTI Strategies for Secondary Teachers*. London: Sage Publications.

Friend, M. (2014a). Collaborative Planning : Realistic Options for Today ' s Educators. In *21st Annual Inclusion Works Conference* (pp. 1–9). Arlington.

Friend, M. (2014b). Face to Face Communication: It's Still Essential, It Still Takes Skill. In *21st Annual Inclusion Works Conference*. Arlington.

Furukawa, J. (1978). Chunking Method of Teaching and Studying: II. *Annual Meeting of the American Psychological*. Toronto, Canada.

Gauthier, I. (2010). Teaching and Evaluating All at Once: Asking Students to Write Their Own Questions | Center for Teaching | Vanderbilt University. Retrieved February 2, 2017, from https://cft.vanderbilt.edu/2010/07/teaching-and-evaluating-all-at-once-asking-students-to-write-their-own-questions/

Gfeller, K. E. (1983). Musical Mnemonics as an Aid to Retention with Normal and

Learning Disabled Students. *Journal of Music Therapy, 20,* 179–189.

Giangreco, M. F., Edelman, S. W., & Broer, S. M. (2001). Respect, Appreciation, and Acknowledgment of Paraprofessionals Who Support Students with Disabilities. *Exceptional Children, 67*(4), 485–498.

Glasser, W. (1999). *Choice theory: A new psychology of personal freedom. Choice theory: A new psychology of personal freedom.* New York: HarperPerennial.

Gonzalez-Cabezas, C., Anderson, O. S., Wright, M. C., & Fontana, M. (2015). Association Between Dental Student-Developed Exam Questions and Learning at Higher Cognitive Levels. *Journal of Dental Education, 79*(11), 1295–304.

Gregory, G., & Kuzmich, L. (2007). *Teacher teams that get results : 61 strategies for sustaining and renewing professional learning communities.* Thousand Oaks: Corwin Press.

Hall, R. H., & Sidio-Hall, M. A. (1994). The Effect of Student Color Coding of Knowledge Maps and Test Anxiety on Student Learning. *The Journal of Experimental Education, 62*(4), 291–302. http://doi.org/10.1080/00220973.1994.9944136

Hayes, B. K., Heit, E., & Rotello, C. M. (2014). Memory, reasoning, and categorization: Parallels and common mechanisms. *Frontiers in Psychology, 5*(JUN), 1–9. http://doi.org/10.3389/fpsyg.2014.00529

Healy, J. M. (1999). *Endangered Minds: Why Children Dont Think And What We Can Do About It* (2nd ed.). New York, N.Y., N.Y.: Simon & Schuster.

Horn, S. (2004). Use "Tongue Fu!" to get along better with teachers, principals, students and parents. *CurriculumReview, 44 (2)*(October), 14–16.

Jausovec, N., Jausovec, K., & Gerlic, I. (2006). The influence of Mozart's music on brain activity in the process of learning. *Clinical Neurophysiology : Official Journal of the International Federation of Clinical Neurophysiology, 117*(12), 2703–2714. http://doi.org/10.1016/j.clinph.2006.08.010

Kennedy, M.J., Thomas, C.N., Meyer,J.P., Alves, K.D., Lloyd, J. W. (2014). Using Evidence-Based Multimedia to Improve Vocabulary Performance of Adolescents with LD: A UDL Approach. *Learning Disability Quarterly, 37*(2). http://doi.org/10.1177/0731948713507262

Kennedy, M. J., Romig, J., & Rodgers, W. J. (2015). Using Content Acquisition Podcasts (CAPs) to Improve Vocabulary Instruction and Learning for Students with Disabilities and Their Teachers. In *Comprehensive Individualized Curriculum and Instructional Design.* Portland: Portland State University Library.

Kohn, A. (1993). Choices for Children: Why and How to Let Students Decide. *Phi Delta Kappan, 75*(1), 8–16,18–21 Sep 1993.

Kriegeskorte, N., Goebel, R., & Bandettini, P. (2006). Information-based functional brain mapping. *Proceedings of the National Academy of Sciences of the United States of America, 103*(10), 3863–8. http://doi.org/10.1073/pnas.0600244103

Kriston, A. (2016). Nonlinguistic Representations and Digital Resources in Vocabulary Teaching. *Scientific Bulletin of the Politehnica University of*

Timişoara, *15*(1), 81–89.

Lah, N. C., Saat, R. M., & Hassan, R. (2014). Cognitive strategy in learning chemistry: How chunking and learning get together. *Malaysian Online Journal of Educational Science*, *2*(1), 9–15.

Marzano, R. J. (2010a). The Art and Science of Teaching/Representing Knowledge Nonlinguistically. *Educational Leadership*, *67*(8), 84–86.

Marzano, R. J. (2010b). The Art and Science of Teaching / When Students Track Their Progress. *Educational Leadership*, *67*(4), 86–87.

Marzano Debra J. Pollock, Jane E., R. J. P., Marzano, R. J., Pickering, D. J., & Pollock, J. E. (2001). *Classroom Instruction That Works: research-based strategies for increasing student achievement*. Alexandria, VA: Association for Supervision and Curriculum Development.

Mastropieri, M. A., & Scruggs, T. E. (1998). Enhancing School Success with Mnemonic Strategies. *Intervention in School and Clinic*. http://doi.org/10.1177/105345129803300402

Mcduffie, K. A., Mastropieri, M., & Scruggs, T. E. (2009). Differential Effects of Peer Tutoring in Co-Taught and Non-Co -Taught Classes: Results for Content Learning and Student- Teacher Interactions. *Exceptional Children*, *75*(4), 493–510.

McGlynn, K., & Kozlowski, J. (2016). Empowering Students Through DATA-2. *Science Scope*, *40*(4), 64–67.

McKeachie, W. J. (1995). Learning Styles Can Become Learning Strategies. *The National Teaching & Learning Forum*, *4*(6), 1–12. http://doi.org/10.1002/ntlf.10024

McVay, P. (1998). Paraprofessionals in the classroom: What role do they play? *Disability Solutions*, *3*(1), 2–4.

Munk, D. D., & Bursuck, W. D. (1998). Report Card Grading Adaptations for Students with Disabilities. *Intervention in School and Clinic*, *33*(5), 306–308. http://doi.org/10.1177/105345129803300508

O'Brien, B., Mansfield, S. J., & Legge, G. E. (2005). The effect of print size on reading speed in dyslexia. *October*, *28*(3), 332–349.

O'Donnell King, Alison, A. M., O'Donnell, A. M., King, A., O'Donnell King, Alison, A. M., O'Donnell, A. M., King, A., ... King, A. (1999). *Cognitive perspectives on peer learning. The Rutgers invitational symposium on education series*. Mahwah: L. Erlbaum.

Oberauer, K., & Hein, L. (2012). Attention to Information in Working Memory. *Current Directions in Psychological Science*, *21*(3), 164–169. http://doi.org/10.1177/0963721412444727

Oei, N. Y. L., Everaerd, W. T. A. M., Elzinga, B. M., van Well, S., & Bermond, B. (2006). Psychosocial stress impairs working memory at high loads: an association with cortisol levels and memory retrieval. *Stress (Amsterdam, Netherlands)*, *9*(3), 133–141. http://doi.org/10.1080/10253890600965773

Ogle, D. M. (1986). K-W-L: A teaching model that develops active reading of expository text. *Reading Teacher*, *39564–570*.

Org, N., Caine, R. N., & Caine, G. (n.d.). The 12 Brain/Mind Natural Learning Principles Expanded 12 Brain/Mind Natural Learning Principles.

Ozcelik, E., Karakus, T., Kursun, E., & Cagiltay, K. (2009). An eye-tracking study of how color coding affects multimedia learning. *Computers and Education*, *53*(2), 445–453. http://doi.org/10.1016/j.compedu.2009.03.002

Palincsar, A. S., & Herrenkohl, L. R. (2002). Designing Collaborative Learning Contexts. *Theory into Practice*, *41*(1), pages 26-32.

Polloway, E. A., Epstein, M. H., Bursuck, W. D., Roderique, T. W., McConeghy, J. L., & Jayanthi, M. (1994). Classroom Grading. *Journal for Special Educators*, *15*(3), 162–170. http://doi.org/10.1177/074193259401500304

Robert, T. (2008). Migraines at Work? Check the Lighting. Retrieved January 1, 2008, from http://www.healthcentral.com/migraine/triggers-160927-5_pf.html

Romain, T., & Verdick, E. (2000). *Stress can really get on your nerves!* Minneapolis: Free Spirit Publications.

Rowe, M. B. (1986). Wait Time: Slowing Down May Be A Way of Speeding Up! *Journal of Teacher Education*, *37*(1), 43–50. http://doi.org/10.1177/002248718603700110

Sadler-Smith, E., & Riding, R. (1999). Cognitive style and instructional preferences. *Instructional Science*, *27*(5), 355–371.

Salmelin, R., Baillet, S., & Leahy, R. M. (2009). Electromagnetic brain imaging. *Human Brain Mapping*, *30*(6), 1753–7. http://doi.org/10.1002/hbm.20795

Siple, P., Caccamise, F., & Brewer, L. (1982). Signs as pictures and signs as words: effect of language knowledge on memory for new vocabulary. *Journal of Experimental Psychology Learning Memory and Cognition*, *8*(6), 619–625.

Sleep, S. (2008). Blue Lighting Up The Human Brain At Work, (11), 2007–2008.

Terregrossa, R. A., Englander, F., & Wang, Z. (2010). How Student Achievement is Related to Student Behaviors and Learning Style Preferences. *International Journal of Education Research*, *5*(2), 94–108.

Vandewalle, G., Schwartz, S., Grandjean, D., Wuillaume, C., Balteau, E., Degueldre, C., ... Maquet, P. (2010). Spectral quality of light modulates emotional brain responses in humans. *Proceedings of the National Academy of Sciences of the United States of America*, *107*(45), 19549–54. http://doi.org/10.1073/pnas.1010180107

Vedhara, K., Hyde, J., Gilchrist, I. D., Tytherleigh, M., & Plummer, S. (2000). Acute stress, memory, attention and cortisol. *Psychoneuroendocrinology*, *25*(6), 535–549. http://doi.org/10.1016/S0306-4530(00)00008-1

Wallace, W. T. (1994). Memory for music: Effect of melody on recall of text. *Journal of Experimental Psychology: Learning, Memory, Cognition*, *20*, 1471–1485.

Webb, M. (1987). *Peer Helping Relationships in Urban Schools. Eric Digest.* New York: ERIC Clearinghouse on Urban Education.

What is a Gifted Child? Trying to define the beast. (2007). Retrieved January 1, 2008, from http://www.nswagtc.org.au/info/definitions/index.html

Whatley, J. (2009). Ground Rules in Team Projects: Findings from a Prototype

System to Support Students. *Journal of Information Technology Education, 8,* 161–176.

Wong, B. (2010). Points of view: Color coding. *Nature Methods, 7*(8), 573–573. http://doi.org/10.1038/nmeth0810-573

Wong, B. (2011). Points of view: Layout. *Nature Methods, 8*(10), 783–783. http://doi.org/10.1038/nmeth.1711

Wright, J. (2011). Using PowerPoint Timers to Improve Student Behavior and Learning. Retrieved September 11, 2016, from http://www.jimwrightonline.com/pdfdocs/timers/timers_intv_ideas.pdf

Wubbolding, R. E. (2007). Glasser Quality School. *Group Dynamics: Theory, Research, and Practice.* http://doi.org/10.1037/1089-2699.11.4.253

Zimmerman, B. J., Bandura, A., & Martinez-Pons, M. (1992). Self-Motivation for Academic Attainment: The Role of Self-Efficacy Beliefs and Personal Goal Setting. *American Educational Research Journal, 29*(3), 663–676. http://doi.org/10.3102/00028312029003663

At the time of the publication of this book, the information cited within is the most current available and/or the original source material. All information has been verified as of January 2017. The author and publisher do not provide any guarantee or warranty regarding the information provided by any sources cited here, nor do we take responsibility for any changes to information or web sites that may occur after verification. If you find an error or would like to alert us to a change to any resource cited herein, please contact us online: http://susanfitzell.com/contact-susan-fitzell/

NOTES

NOTES

_____

_____

_____

_____

_____

_____

_____

_____

_____

_____

_____

_____

_____

_____

_____

_____

_____

_____

_____

_____

_____

NOTES

About the Author

Susan Gingras Fitzell, M.Ed., CSP, has been consulting, writing, and presenting since 1993 and has spent the past 15 years onsite in organizations throughout the United States working hand- in-hand with teachers, management, and employees helping them to increase productivity, learning, and problem solving to reach their goals.

She has authored over a dozen books and is one of only 650 certified speaking professionals in the world today. Susan is a dynamic, nationally recognized speaker as well as an innovative change agent, compassionate coach, and effective productivity & learning expert. After working with Susan, clients are more efficient, productive, and effective.

She is a black belt in kickboxing and a student of kung fu. Her family prides themselves in being geeks and her two adult children have both earned degrees in mechanical engineering using the strategies that Susan shares with her clients.

Other selected titles by Susan Gingras Fitzell, M.Ed.:
- 100+ Tech Ideas for Teaching English and Language Arts
- Co-Teaching and Collaboration in the Classroom: Strategies for Success
- Free The Children: Conflict Education for Strong & Peaceful Minds
- Memorization and Test Taking Strategies
- Motivating Students to Choose Success
- Paraprofessionals and Teachers Working Together
- Please Help Me with My Homework! Strategies for Parents and Caregivers (English and Spanish)
- RTI Strategies for Secondary Teachers
- Transforming Anger to Personal Power: An Anger Management Curriculum for Grades 6 through 12
- Umm Studying? What's That? Learning Strategies for the Overwhelmed and Confused College and High School Student
- Use iPads and Other Cutting-Edge Technology to Strengthen Your Instruction

Bring Susan to Your School for Consultation or In-Service

Susan Fitzell, M.Ed., CSP, has nearly 25 years of expertise as a teacher, educational consultant, and leadership coach. She is a sought-after speaker, educating and inspiring thousands each year and is the author of over a dozen books on collaborative teaching, ed-tech, learning strategies, & inclusion.

Susan's keynotes and workshops are interactive, content rich, dynamic presentations. She customizes to meet her clients' needs to ensure relevance to the client organizations' dynamics.

Choose from four customizable topics:

Motivating Students to Choose Success
Learn practical strategies to motivate your students to make positive choices, put forth their best effort, & realize they are in control of their own destiny.

Co-teaching & Collaboration for All
Maximize the skills of co-teachers & specialists in your inclusive classrooms with NEW, concrete implementation approaches that take the guesswork out of collaboration.

Differentiation Strategy Blast
Discover a variety of brain-based, research supported, "implement tomorrow" strategies that maintain rigor, maximize time, and increase success for all learners.

Paraprofessionals and Teachers Working Together
Four mini-workshops in one day to strengthen critical skills needed for success in the classroom.: 1. Build a Strong Foundation for Success, 2. How to Collaborate Successfully, 3. Positive Behavior Management and 4. Academic Support

Launch your conference or benefit with Susan's Keynote:
Differentiated Instruction: Why Bother? Aka: Inclusion: Why Bother? Shift mind-sets that challenge successful differentiated instruction and inclusive practices. The motto of this powerful keynote is "Good for all, critical for the students with special needs."

Bring Instructional Strategies or Co-teaching UP a Level with Coaching Support
Coaching Session Options

Option One: Coaching Session

1. Individual teacher identifies concerns and best possible outcome.
2. Teacher requests consultant to
   - Observe X, Y, or Z within the classroom.
   - Suggest strategies and techniques to address concerns.
3. Set up follow-up time
4. Consultant & teacher discuss options available to address concerns.
5. Teacher implements new strategies.
6. Consultant follows up with teacher to provide ongoing support.

Option Two: Materials Adaptation

1. Teacher comes to session with lesson plan and all materials required to implement the lesson.
2. Consultant works with the teacher to identify and where possible prepare simple adaptations to meet student Individual Education Plan needs.

Option Three: Co-planning: Chunking Lesson Plans™

1. Co-teachers come to session with lesson plan goals and all materials required to plan the lesson.
2. Consultant works with co-teachers to plan together taking into consideration professional roles in the classroom as well as multiple ability levels. Co-teachers are encouraged and coached to contribute "both" their ideas for creating or enhancing a lesson plan.

   NOTE: *Coaching sessions are NON-EVALUATIVE. Confidentiality is always maintained.*

IF YOU DIDN'T DO IT YET, DON'T FORGET
GET YOUR BONUS RESOURCES HERE:

http://Bonus367.susanfitzell.com

DID YOU FIND A TYPO?

Although this document has been thoroughly reviewed and edited, there is always a chance that we missed something. If you find a typo or other issue in this book, send it to me in email at sfitzell@susanfitzell.com and you will be entered into our monthly prize drawing!

School Professional Development License Agreement

This AimHi Educational Programs, LLC license agreement is subject to change without notice. It is the users' responsibility to check the license agreement prior to conducting training.

The licensing agreement can be found here:

license.susanfitzell.com

Made in the USA
Columbia, SC
23 July 2021